NESSIPEES

Nessey's Recipes for Life, Liberty, & the Pursuit of Wholeness

NESSIPEES

Nessey's Recipes for Life, Liberty, & the Pursuit of Wholeness

NEW YORK CITY - PHOENIX - MIDLAND

This edition Published by

Copyright© Rising Monarch Press 2013

All rights reserved. No part of this publication may be reproduced, stored in a retrieval system or transmitted, in any form or by any means, electronic, mechanical, photocopying, recording or otherwise, without the prior permission of the copyright holder.

ISBN 978-0-615-76416-0

Printed in the United States of America
by Epic Print Solutions

Photographs of Nessey's Recipes by Benjamin Blackketter

Graphic Design of the Book, Cover, and Layout by Matt Harnly

"Nessey Tip" Angel illustrated/graphic by Dianne Bianchi

"Traveling Butterfly" illustrated by Jenness,
converted to graphic by Matt Harnly

"Honor the Lord with your substance, and with the firstfruits of all your increase."

(PROVERBS 3:9 KJV)

··

I dedicate this book, my firstfruits, to the Lord Jesus Christ, my Daddy, Friend, and Companion.

Thank You for the Journey of making this project.

Glorify Yourself through my meager offering to Your people.

Table of Contents

NOTE FROM THE AUTHOR

1: Purpose 1

2: 21Days 1

3: Appendix 2

4: Title 2

21 Days:

   1. ABUNDANT LIFE/Applesauce Muffins (Y2F) 6

   2. PARDONED!/Peanut Butter Balls (YK) 9

   3. IT COMES WITH BENEFITS/Mom's Squash Muffins, Nessey Style (YF) 11

   4. SPREAD YOUR WINGS AND FLY!/Oatmeal Bread (Y2F) 13

   5. GROWING/Coconoat Flatbread (Nessey's Hummus) (Y2F/YK) 15

   6. NO MORE RULES!/Brownies (Y2F) 19

   7. THE ONE WHO LEADS ME/Blonde Brownies (Y2F) 21

   8. DID I MISS YOU?/Nessey's Nuts: Sugar 'N Spice (YK) 31

   9. GIFT OF FAITH/Nessey's Nuts: Texas Spice (YK) 33

  10. FAITH TO WAIT IN THE STORM/"Sugar" Cookies (YF) 35

  11. DISAPPOINTED HOPE/Soft Peanut Butter Cookies (YK) 39

  12. SUFFERING FOR RIGHTEOUSNESS/Nessey's Nutty Cookies (YF) 43

  13. THE COFFIN/Christmas Cookies (Hot Cocoa) (Y2F/YK) 45

  14. IMMOVEABLE MOUNTAINS/ "Tea-Time" Spice Cakes (YK) 49

  15. SHELVED BUT HELD/Traditional Yellow Cake (Powder-Puff Frosting) (YF/YK) 58

  16. SUFFICIENT GRACE/Coco-Cupcakes (YF) 63

  17. THE JOY OF TRIBULATION/5 Flavored Pound Cake (YF) 67

  18. IN THE WILL/Nessey's Vanilla Ice Cream (YF) 69

  19. BLESSED OBEDIENCE/Nessey's Coco-Fudge Pie (Pie Crusts) (YF/YF) 73

      Nessey's Heavy Cream/Almond Pastry Crust (YF/YF) 77

20. THE WORST OF TIMES ARE THE BEST OF TIMES/Nessey's Peanut Butter Pie (YF) 79

21. CATALYST/Carrot Pie (Y2F) 83

EPILOGUE: IN LIGHT OF ETERNITY 87

APPENDIX: 90

Endnotes 91

Bibliography 93

Nutrition Facts 95

Prologue 104

Introduction to Yeast-Free Eating

   1. What is Yeast 106

   2. Labeling (YK; YF; Y2F) 106

   3. Nessey Tips 107

   4. Devotionals 107

Nessey's Good Housekeeping Guide

   1. Tips for Cooking 109

   2. Measurement Guide 110

   3. Storing 110

Brands 111

Acknowledgements 113

About Nessey 115

Other Titles by the Author 117

Note from the

First of all, I want to thank you for taking the time to read through this book. I am humbled that you would honor me with the privilege of reading through my work, and my dearest wish is that you will be ABUNDANTLY blessed by the information you receive as your eyes graze each page.

Secondly, allow me to explain the purpose of this book, and the inspiration for the title.

PURPOSE: First, a little background to the creation of this book. When I first began this project, I was hoping to create a book, in which I could "feed" the entire individual: body, soul, and spirit. However, I wanted to focus primarily on the "physical" aspect; I wished to write a "cookbook," in which I could share recipes I had created specifically modified for the special dietary needs innate with the complications of my health issues. Then, I desired to include throughout the book several of my devotional articles I had written over the course of my illness that discuss different insights and revelations, which I had received during my journey through affliction. However, as the project developed, I came to realize that I had far more devotional articles than I did recipes. Moreover, I discovered countless cookbooks with similar health guidelines (yeast-free eating) that included extensive numbers of recipes, health guides and tools, etc. that FAR surpassed my own – in short, I found my project a dismal attempt to bring helpful eating tips to anyone, in comparison with so many far superior, and astronomically more thorough, cookbooks that could offer an enormously better guide for the yeast-free eater. Trying to insert my cookbook among these "health book giants" would have been like a flea demanding attention from an elephant herd.

At any rate, a change in tactic was in order. At the suggestion of wise counsel, I switched the primary focus of this project from "physical food" to "spiritual food." My initial idea was (and is) still in hand: my aspiration to "feed" the entire person, body, soul, and spirit, remains the agenda. However, this book is by no means a cookbook, nor is it a "yeast-free" encyclopedia. It is a devotional book, containing some of the fruit of God's labor of His Work in and through me, the comfort He Himself has given me as He has gently guided me through long years of suffering, comfort which He desires for others to receive and cherish.

> My aspiration to "feed" the entire person, body, soul, and spirit, is still the agenda.

21 DAYS: Inside, you will find 21 devotionals and 21 recipes, a three week journey of "eternal feasting," birthed from my spirit and displayed on the following pages – both spiritual and physical food for your soul and body to enjoy. Why 21 days? Aside from the fact that I've only invented 21 yeast-free recipes (kidding), there is great Spiritual significance to that time frame. Daniel fasted and prayed for 21 days, refraining from the consumption of sweet meats and wines, resulting in a visit from an angel, who shared a glorious prophetic revelation of future events (Dan. 10:1-13). In addition, I happily discovered that, in Hebraic culture, the Feast of Unleavened Bread (i.e. Unleavened meaning "Yeast-

Author

Free") requires a 7 day fast to take place during the 14th through 21st days of the first month, prior to the actual feast (Ex. 12:26). With these Biblical references, why not have a 21 day spiritual journey with "unleavened" recipes for soul and body?

APPENDIX: You will find an extensive Appendix at the end of the book. This appendix includes more thorough explanatory information about yeast in general, as well as recipe instructions, cooking ideas, and helpful tips that are directly associated with the recipes you find. It also contains a little information about my personal yeast issues, and can be used as a guide tool for any reader, who has, or has had, similar struggles with yeast problems.

TITLE: The name *NESSIPEES: Nessey's Recipes for Life, Liberty, & the Pursuit of Wholeness*, is first, a merging of my nickname "Ness" and the word "Recipes." Secondly, it is inspired by the message of Phil. 3:12-14:

"Not that I have already ... been made perfect, but I press on to take hold of that for which Christ Jesus took hold of me. Brothers, I do not consider myself yet to have taken hold of it. But one thing I do: Forgetting what is behind and straining toward what is ahead, I press on toward the goal to win the prize for which God has called me heavenward in Christ Jesus."

Christ came for several reasons, among which are the following: to give us LIFE to the full until it overflows (Jn. 10:10), to LIBERATE us from the curse of sin and death (Rom. 8:2), to heal us and make us WHOLE and complete in Him, lacking nothing (Eph. 4:13; Jms. 1:4).

When we accept Jesus Christ as our Savior, we are endowed with "automatic" gifts: new LIFE in and through Him, and the assurance of eternal life following our physical death. Moreover, we are given LIBERTY, or freedom from the bondage of sin. However, we are not automatically made "WHOLE" in our persons upon our salvation because wholeness (that inner healing of our hearts, minds, souls, and sometimes even our bodies from the wounds, consequences, and ramifications of living in a dark world) is achieved over the course of our *journeys* of pursuing a deeper, more intimate relationship with

> We have life and liberty in Him, and we will ALWAYS be pursuing wholeness as we walk with Him in this life.

Christ. Therefore, we have life and liberty in Him, and we will ALWAYS be pursuing wholeness as we walk with Him in this life.

The contents of this project are merely some spiritual and physical "recipes" designed to remind you of your Life and Liberty you already have *in* Christ, and to assist you on your journey toward wholeness in spirit, soul, and body.

May the Lord BLESS you as you read this book! May you be encouraged, nourished, uplifted, and wholly fulfilled as you "feast" your whole self on the information you are about to receive. May *NESSIPEES* equip your heart, soul, body, and spirit to live your life on this side of heaven in complete victory and abundance!

WEEK One

Abundant Life

Day 1

The thief comes only in order to steal and kill and destroy. I came that you may have and enjoy life, and have it in abundance [to the full, till it overflows].

(John 10:10 AMP)

What is abundant life? What does it mean to have life to the full until it overflows? What does it mean to live a "good life"? Does it mean that we never face heartache or troubles? Does it mean we live a life of lollipops and Disneyland? By no means!

How can you appreciate the sun unless you've experienced the rain? How do you know what joy is unless you've felt sorrow? What is night if it is not contrasted by day? How could you enjoy your favorite meal/dessert/beverage unless you'd eaten something you couldn't stand? What is success unless there is failure?

We have to get off of this mindset that "good" is all whip cream and fluff. "Good" is so much deeper than the surface of happiness and ease. Think about some scenarios. We all know it's "good" to eat our vegetables, why? Because they offer vital nutrients to our bodies. We know that it's "good" to exercise and workout, why? Because it strengthens our muscles and builds our immune systems, enhancing our overall sense of wellbeing. But who ever said eating your greens was easy? Who hasn't experienced some type of soreness, waddling up and down stairs, after a hard workout?!

There is no victory without overcoming some obstacle or enemy, right? Moreover, you can't "win" unless you've fought against an opponent, who was bent on making you lose.

It's "good" to win; it's "good" to feel "good;" it's "good" to eat your favorite meal; it's "good" to succeed … but "good" is not just the victory – it includes the pain it took to win it. "Good" is not just the success – it intimates the failure you overcame to achieve it.

Yes, Christ said that He came to give us abundant life, but He also said, *"In this world you will have trouble. But take heart! I have overcome the world"* (Jn. 16:33). Trouble comes in this life that Christ overcame – it's part of the picture of abundant life. Abundant life is more than a life of ease – it is a life of victory, conquering, and overcoming. But these three things are only obtained by having to face and defeat trouble, heartache, pain, and trial. We have an abundant life in Christ – and it means walking the road He walked … a road of victory *over* pain and trouble.

"… in all these things we are more than conquerors through Him who loved us …" (Rom. 8:37)

Applesauce Muffins

Applesauce Muffins | Y2F

- **1/2 c.** Xylosweet *(Xylitol sweetener - packed)*
- **1-1/2 c.** Flaxseed Meal *(Bob's Red Mill)*
- **1-1/2 c.** Org. Oat Flour *(Arrowhead Mills)*
- **1-1/2 tsp.** Baking Soda
- **1/2 tsp.** Salt
- **2** Eggs
- **1 c.** Org. Unsweetened Applesauce
- **4 Tbsp.** Coconut Oil

Preheat oven to 400° F.

Grease muffin cups
(Or use paper muffin cups).

Blend dry ingredients together well.
Add eggs one at a time; blend well.
Add applesauce; blend.
Melt coconut oil, then add to mixture.
Blend all ingredients well.

Spoon batter into muffin cups.
Bake 18 min. or until toothpick comes out clean.

Makes 12 muffins.

Nessey TIPS

For a fun addition, fill the muffin cup halfway with the mix, then place a Peanut Butter Ball (see pg. 10) in the middle, and then cover it with more mix (filling the muffin cup). The Peanut Butter Ball will bake with the muffin, and you'll have a fun tasty surprise in the middle of your yummy treat!

Pardoned!

Day 2

When you were dead in your sins and in the uncircumcision of your sinful nature, God made you alive with Christ. He forgave us all our sins ...
(Col. 2:13)

What does it mean to be circumcised from our sinful nature? How are we made alive in Christ and what does it mean to be forgiven of *all* of our sins?

In the Old Testament, God required the Israelites to circumcise all males. This was done to symbolically distinguish them as God's chosen people. Anyone who was *un*circumcised was considered a Gentile or pagan, those who practiced "lawlessness" and *not* citizens of Israel. Before we accept Jesus as Savior, we are "uncircumcised" in our souls. We willfully sin and rebel with little conscience, lost in our own abyss of wrongs. When Christ comes to live within us, we become "circumcised" in spirit. We are washed clean of all of our sins, forgiven of the life we lived before salvation, and secured into God's family as His chosen people through Christ.

Imagine Saddam Hussein in his Iraqi jail cell days before his execution. Guilty of multiple war crimes, such as genocide and other horrific murderous plots, Hussein continues to rant and rave hateful threats, completely unashamed of his life and unchanged in his behavior. Now imagine Former President Bush coming to visit Hussein. Stepping into the cell and taking a seat directly across from his enemy, Bush presents an unthinkable proposal. He offers to release Hussein from his prison sentence, completely pardon every crime he has ever committed, and totally wipe out his criminal record. Bush promises all of this and more if Hussein would become a U.S. citizen.

It sounds like an outrageous scenario, but did you know that that is exactly what Christ does for us? We are overwhelmingly guilty of sin and shame; we are

> Christ comes to us, sits down with us in the midst of our messes, and offers complete forgiveness of sin and renewal.

stuck in our prison of sinful, filthy hearts and minds. Even so, *while* we are locked in our own sinful ways, Christ comes to us, sits down with us in the midst of our messes, and offers complete forgiveness of sin and renewal of soul if we will simply believe in Him. It is when we accept this amazing offer of salvation that we are "circumcised" into the Body of Christ, no longer pagans or sinners, but children of God. Our record of wrongs is forgiven and wiped clean, and we become God's chosen people, citizens of Heaven.

Peanut Butter Balls

YK

2 c. (or one 16oz. jar) Unsweetened Crunchy/Roasted Peanut Butter

3 to **3-1/2 c.** Almond Flour

1/2 c. Xylosweet

1/2 c. Chopped Nuts

Mix the peanut butter, almond flour, nuts, and Xylosweet in a bowl until it becomes a "doughy" mixture.

On wax paper, spread more Xylosweet. Take pieces of the mix and roll into quarter size balls, then coat them with the sweetener.

Store the balls in a Tupperware container, and place in freezer: allow to freeze overnight. Keep balls in freezer as a frozen treat, or for use in other recipes (see Applesauce Muffins for details).

Nessey TIPS

Want to try a tasty variation? For a subtle and lighter taste, use unsweetened almond butter and chopped almond pieces instead. Another variation: for a richer savor, try unsweetened cashew butter with cashew pieces. For any variation, when you use raw creamy nut butters, the balls have a "smoother, softer" taste. The roasted crunchy varieties offer a bolder experience.

It Comes with Benefits

Day 3

So then, just as you received Christ Jesus as Lord, continue to live in Him, rooted and built up in Him, strengthened in the faith as you were taught, and overflowing with thankfulness. (Col. 2:6-7)

When we accept Jesus Christ as our Lord, we receive a remarkable gift. Not only do we receive the salvation from our sins, but we also are immediately adopted into the Heavenly family of the King of Heaven, which comes with an abundant package of supreme benefits.[1] We are given authority in high places,[2] an inheritance of supernatural blessings,[3] and complete access to the Divine Counselor 24 hours of every day![4] We receive all of this and more the moment we say, "Jesus, come into my heart." But you might say, "Well, I'm a Christian, but I am *not* seeing all of these 'benefits' in my life."

How do we access these promises of God? What does Scripture say? "*Just as you have received Christ, continue to live in Him …*" Salvation occurs when we accept Jesus Christ as Lord, but it is only the *beginning* of our Christianity. After we accept His salvation, we must also accept His relationship as our Father, Brother, and Friend. "*… rooted and built up in Him …*" Relationships are formed through daily fellowship. We are rooted in Christ's family, but we must *build* our relationship with Christ through our daily walk with Him in prayer, Bible study, and Christian fellowship. "*… strengthened in the faith as you were taught …*" As we develop our relationship with Christ, we grow stronger in our faith and maturity as believers. "*… and overflowing with thankfulness …*" While we "grow up" in the family of God, we will begin to see the amazing benefits of His presence and overflow with a thankful heart!

Say someone gives you a car. Not just any car, but the top-grade, Cadillac luxury Escalade, with Bose sound system, leather interior, premium horsepower CAR! What an incredible gift! You have the title deed and the keys are in your pocket … what do you do? You take that machine out for a spin! You get familiar with all of its features, turn up the volume on the stereo, maybe even speed a little to get a "feel" for the acceleration. It's *your* car and you get to *know* your car! It's the same way with Christ. He is the best gift we could ever receive. With Him, we have an abundance of blessings and promises beyond our wildest dreams![5]

You've got the keys, the Holy Spirit. Go take Jesus out for a spin and get to know your Savior and King!

Mom's Squash Muffins
NesseyStyle

YF

2 lbs. (4-6)	Yellow Squash
2	Eggs
1 c.	Butter, melted
1 c.	Xylosweet
1-1/4 c.	Coconut Flour
1 tsp.	Salt
1 Tbsp. + 2 tsp.	Baking Powder

Preheat oven to 375° F.

Wash squash thoroughly; trim off ends. Cut squash into pieces and steam until tender. Puree in food processor, then measure 2 cups of mashed squash.

In a bowl, combine squash, eggs, and butter. Stir well then set aside.

Mix dry ingredients in a large bowl, and make a well in the center. Pour wet mix into the well of the dry and stir until just moistened. Spoon batter into muffin cups (about ¾ full).

Bake for 20 – 25 min. or until toothpick comes out clean. Serves great with stews, steaks, and other "meat hearty" meals.

Nessey TIPS

My Mom makes THE BEST muffins in the ENTIRE WORLD!!! Her delectable delight shames even the most mouthwatering cornbreads and buttermilk biscuits ... but, they're not yeast-free. Miraculously, I was able to remedy this misfortune and create a "Nessey Version" of Mom's recipe. Though it's not "Mom's" exactly (after all, it's impossible to change perfection and have perfect results), it's perty darn close! Enjoy!!!

Spread Your Wings and Fly!

Day 4

Since, then, you have been raised with Christ, set your hearts on things above, where Christ is seated at the right hand of God.

(Col. 3:1)

After we are saved, there is a great temptation to think about and feel guilty over our pasts. But Jesus does not want us to be consumed by the condemning thoughts of our former lives. We have been raised out of our sin. Christ desires for us to focus all our thoughts on Him, *see* Him as the Savior who sits high upon Heaven's throne, reflect upon His *goodness* towards us, and *enjoy* the new life that He has *now* given us.

Look at a butterfly. Its colors are radiant; its wings glisten in the sun as it dances through the air, gracefully gliding to and fro. It flies so joyfully and freely as if it were singing to the music of its own inner song. But the butterfly was not always so beautiful. In fact, it was the farthest from anything desirable or pleasant. It began its life as a worm. A squishy, slimy larva that oozed its way up and down plant stems, feasting on dirt and grime. But, do you think the butterfly reflects on those days? Certainly not! It has been completely transformed into a new creation; it will never be a worm again! It spends its time soaring in beautiful array, feasting on the sweet pollen of elegant flowers!

The same happens when we ask Jesus to take over our lives. We are completely recreated in Christ as a new creature![1] We are not who we were before we met Jesus. We are reborn, sanctified, and made anew by the Blood of Christ![2] Can you imagine a butterfly, as beautiful as it is, staying on the ground, never spreading its wings, and continuing to eat the grime of its former life? Then, how can we, the righteousness of God in Christ,[3] possibly try to "relive" in our minds the old ways of our flesh? We are no longer those people and will never be again! We are dead to sin and alive to Christ Jesus![4]

Stop thinking about your past. Look to the Christ of your present. Take your example from the butterfly; spread your wings and fly!

Oatmeal Bread

Y2F

1-1/4 c.	Boiling Water
1 c.	Steel Cut Oats
1-1/4 c.	Unsweetened Almond Milk
3 Tbsp.	Coconut Oil
3 Tbsp.	Xylosweet
1 tsp.	Salt
2-1/4 c.	Oat Flour
1/2 c.	Coconut Flour

1) In a pot, boil water and then stir in steel cut oats. Turn down heat to low and cover to cook, stirring occasionally, for about 10 min. Cook to level of desired consistency (I prefer gooey, so I cook 10 min., turn off heat, then leave the oatmeal covered to cool, stirring occasionally). Cool to lukewarm.

2) In a skillet, heat milk, oil, Xylosweet, and salt. Pour mixture into oatmeal, stir.

3) Sprinkle in oat flour one cup at a time, stirring in between "pours" (1 c., 1 c., 1/4 c.). Then, sprinkle in coconut flour and stir together (the dough will be sticky). Gather dough together and, to help with stickiness, "powder" dough with a little coconut flour to make one big lump.

4) Grease a loaf pan and spread dough evenly. Preheat oven to 350° F and bake 1 hr. To remove from pan, place foil on the bottom and slowly turn pan upside down to the rack: bread should be in a loaf. Let sit for a few minutes (until it stops steaming). Then, to cool, cover with foil to keep bread moist and soft.

Nessey TIPS

This bread is supposed to be gooey in the middle (like oatmeal) and firm on the outside. It is best kept in an airtight container and refrigerated.

Oatmeal Bread tastes wonderful heated, smothered with almond butter and sprinkled with Xylosweet and cinnamon!

Growing

Day 5

Little by little, you are getting stronger. One of the things that I had to do, when analyzing my overall journey through chronic illness, was not look at the day to day, but rather, look at the year to year progression of strength. For example, one year, in one of my worst seasons of illness, I was in critical condition, scaring doctors, confined to the premise of my home because the literal "stress" and energy it would take to leave would land me in the hospital. I barely had any strength to walk around the house; my life was literally hanging by a thread. Almost exactly one year later, however, I was sitting on a stage singing in an opera! Yes, I was still weak and had to sit, but I was participating in a play! From death's door to performing on stage! What a progression!

All throughout life's journeys, we have to look at the overall picture. The Lord grew in wisdom and stature and favor with both God and men.[1] He didn't just come to earth, born of Mary all suited up with miraculous power, wisdom, etc. ... He had to *grow* from year to year. And if *He* had to grow in strength, the only perfect Man who ever lived, then won't we as well?

Let that encourage you! Look at the years of your trials, and see how you've come from one year to the next. Don't look at the day to day: that can get a little discouraging, especially if your situation is chronic. With ongoing issues, it's almost impossible to see or feel any differences between one day to the next ... until we adopt God's vantage point of the big picture.

Don't only look at the progression of your physical circumstances, though; look at the growth of your *character* and how you've grown in the person you are also! The heartaches and joys we face in the day to day process of suffering are priceless treasures that can only come through trials! That's why James says, "Count it all joy when you face trials and tribulations,"[2] because what is being molded in you is an incredible treasure chest of wonder and glory from the Father alone! And if it's of God, it has to be unimaginably wonderful!

> Your Heavenly Father, Who loves you more than you could possibly fathom, has called you to a divine and awesome purpose. You may not see what it is, but HE does!

Your Heavenly Father, Who loves you more than you could possibly fathom, has called you to a divine and awesome purpose. You may not see what it is, but *HE* does! And it is so so good! He is able to do exceedingly abundantly above all you could ever dare to hope, ask, or think! And those of us, who have been called to walk a road of suffering are in good company! Look at Job, Joseph, Ruth, Daniel, Jeremiah, Paul, and above all, Jesus! Their lives were comprised of suffering, and their rewards were immeasurably great! In fact, the Lord included their stories in the Bible, His *WORD* to use as examples to not only help His people fight the good fight of faith, but to also be used in the very book/letter that shows us who He is! What a remarkable gift!

As we say in our household, "Hang in there," friend! You may not know what God has in store for you, but if you keep walking, keep rejoicing, keep persevering, you will see the goodness of the Lord in the land of the living.

Coconoat Flatbread

Y2F

1-1/4 c.	Boiling Water
1 c.	Steel Cut Oats
1-1/4 c.	Unsweetened Almond Milk
3 Tbsp.	Coconut Oil
3 Tbsp.	Xylosweet
1 tsp.	Salt
1 c.	Coconut Flour

1) In a pot, boil water and then stir in steel cut oats. Turn down heat to low and cover to cook, stirring occasionally, for about 10 min. Cook to level of desired consistency (I prefer gooey, so I cook 10 min., turn off heat, then leave the oatmeal covered to cool, stirring occasionally). Cool to lukewarm.

2) In a skillet, heat milk, oil, Xylosweet, and salt. Pour mixture into oatmeal and stir.

3) Sprinkle coconut flour into oatmeal mix a little at a time, stirring as you pour it in until all is mixed.

4) Preheat oven to 350° F.

5) Grease a pizza platter tray with oil and spread dough evenly. Bake 20 – 25 min. Bring platter out of oven and cover with aluminum foil to cool (this will soften and "glue" the bread together). Once cool, take pizza cutter and slice into squares. The "Flatbread" will be crumbly, so be careful when transferring it to a keeper or to eat. See Nessey Tips for serving suggestions.

Nessey TIPS

The Flatbread should look cracked when you pull it out of the oven. Also, it will be a little crumbly prior to cooling in the fridge. It's a delicate bread regardless, so be careful when transferring it to a keeper or to eat. Best eaten as a finger food. You can eat it plain, or topped with almond butter sprinkled with Xylosweet (one of my favorite treats), or you can serve with Nessey's Hummus (see recipe).

Nessey  TIPS

* When you're draining the can of beans, try to get as much liquid out as possible for a thicker dip. Also, be sure to transfer the beans into the food processor by hand; this prevents any extra liquid mixing into the dip —again, the less extra liquid, the thicker the dip.

** The hummus will mix more evenly if you pour in the ingredients in the order given (starting with liquids).

Nessey's Hummus

YK

1	15oz. Can Chickpeas/Garbanzo Beans	
1/4 c.	Liquid from Can	
2 Tbsp.	Tahini Butter	
2 Tbsp.	Lemon Juice	
1/2 tsp.	Ground Cumin	
1/2 tsp.	Salt	
3/4 tsp.	Granulated Garlic	
	or	
1-1/2	Garlic Cloves *(minced)*	

After removing the ¼ c. liquid, completely drain the can of beans.* In the food processor, combine all ingredients as follows (I start with liquids): ** pour in liquid, then lemon juice, then tahini butter; sprinkle each "powder" ingredient evenly around the liquid; then transfer beans by hand* and sprinkle on top of the other ingredients.

Start processor and let run while you are cleaning up your area (the longer the processor runs, the better the consistency and fluff of final dip). Stop processor and stir in the sides with spoon or mixer, replace lid and start processor again. Let it run another minute or two.

Once mixed, transfer to bowl and serve or refrigerate.

That's why James says, "Count it all joy when you face trials and tribulations," because what is being molded in you is an incredible treasure chest of wonder and glory from the Father alone!

No More Rules!

Day 6

Since you died with Christ to the basic principles of this world, why, as though you still belonged to it, do you submit to its rules ...

(Col. 2:20)

Do you ever feel like you're only "holy" if you *do* something "holy"? You know; you're only a "Good Christian" *if*:

1) You pray 3 hours a day (brownie points if you do it in one sitting)
2) You memorize 12 verses a week
3) You read the whole Bible in a year ...

Such rules are fine; but do they really make us good Christians? Not according to Colossians 2:20.

What else happened when Christ died on the cross? He took the penalty for our sins; but is that *all* that He did? No! He not only took the punishment of sin,[1] but He *also* fulfilled the *Law*.[2] The Law is the set of "religious" rules that requires us to perform sacrifices and rituals so that God would consider us "holy." However, when Christ was crucified as the Perfect Sacrifice, *He* completely satisfied *all* of the religious rules and regulations, and *we* are released from having to worry about them. In Christ, we not only die to our sins, but also to the curse of the Law![3]

Even so, we still feel like we have to perform *some* rules in order to at least *look* holy, right?

Imagine a group of boarding school students all dressed up in their cute little uniforms. The boys have on their suit coats and ties with shirts neatly tucked in. The girls are wearing their pretty dresses with panty hose. They all look so nice from the outside. But in reality, they are all *extremely* uncomfortable. The coats are stuffy, the ties are choking, the hose is scratchy, and the dresses are tight. They are children, known for playfulness and freedom, but they are trapped in their outerwear for the sake of "looking" sharp.

It's the same with us when we try to "look" holy. We get bogged down trying to be "good Christians." We feel like we *have* to pray an hour a day; we *have* to read seven chapters a night; we *have* to do this or that ... but this is not what Christ meant for us! He died so we could have and *enjoy* our lives![4] He already fulfilled the requirements of holiness! We don't have to *do* things to be holy. We *are* holy because Christ *made* us holy.[5]

Put the rulebooks away. Lose the tie. Relax and *enjoy* the good life the Lord has given to you in Christ.

Brownies

Y2F

1 c.	Xylosweet
1-1/2 sticks	Butter
	or
3/4 c.	Coconut Oil
2 Tbsp.	Water
2	Eggs
1 tsp.	Vanilla
1-1/3 c.	Oat Flour
3/4 c.	Unsweetened Baking Cocoa
1/2 tsp.	Baking Powder
1/4 tsp.	Salt
3/4 c.	Chopped Nuts (optional)

Preheat oven to 350° F.

Cream Xylosweet and butter in large mixing bowl. Add water, eggs, and vanilla, and mix well.

In a smaller bowl, mix flour, cocoa, baking powder, and salt. Pour into wet mixture and mix well. (Batter should be thick). Add nuts and continue to mix.

Grease 8x8 or 9x9 baking pan with oil or butter. Pour batter into pan. Bake 18-25 min. or until toothpick comes out clean (in middle of batter).

Nessey TIPS

For a Yeast Free (**YF**) variety, use 3 cups of almond flour instead of the oat flour.

The One Who Leads Me

Day 7

For this God is our God forever and ever;
He will be our Guide even to the end.

(Psalm 48:14)

I have a friend, who I will call "Shannon,"[1] who sees through the eyes of another. That's right; Shannon is blind. But she is not impaired; Shannon has an irreplaceable friend, Nina,[1] a 75lb., 3 year old black lab, who is Shannon's constant companion. Everywhere Shannon goes, her four-legged guide leads her there. Nina is a steady helper, leader, and friend. Nina may be silent, but she is *very* present. Without Nina, Shannon would be completely helpless, unable to do those little things in life that we so often take for granted.

We are not much different than my friend Shannon. Our physical eyes may see just fine, but our spiritual eyes are incapable of seeing into the future, into our life's path, which the Lord has laid out for us. We need a Guide, One who can see His way clearly, and lead us into the plans He has for us.

"*'For I know the plans I have for you,' declares the LORD, 'plans to prosper you and not to harm you, plans to give you hope and a future'*" (Jer. 29:11).

God has many names: Jehovah-Jireh (Our Provider), Jehovah-Nissi (our Banner), Jehovah-Rophi (The One Who Heals). Another name given to Him is the Hebrew name, Nā·hăg,[2] which means "God My Guide" or "The One Who Leads Me." This is the attribute of God that led the people of Israel through the wilderness, providing a cloud by day and fire by night. The Israelites didn't know where they were going; all they had was the Cloud in front of them, Who knew exactly how to get the people of Israel to the Promised Land (see Ex. 13:21-22).

There's something else about Shannon's and Nina's friendship that we have to consider. Shannon also has to *trust* her guide. Nina would not be able to help Shannon "see" her way through life if Shannon didn't allow Nina to *be* her "guiding eyes." It's the same with us. We have to trust our Guide to lead us through all seasons of life; we have to believe that He knows where He's going, even if we can't see our way too well. *He* can see our way clearly, and He *will* lead us in the right path. Trust Him, and allow Him to guide you in the way that pleases Him.

"Trust in the LORD with all your heart ... and He will make your paths straight" (Prov. 3:5-6).

Blonde Brownies

Y2F

1-1/4 c.	Whole Oats *(Quaker - see Brands)*
1/2 tsp.	Salt
1 tsp.	Baking Soda
1/2 c.	Coconut Oil
1-1/4 c.	Xylosweet
2	Eggs
1 tsp.	Vanilla Extract
1 tsp.	Butter Extract
1-16 oz. jar	Unsweetened Peanut Butter

Preheat oven to 350° F.

In a small bowl, mix oats, salt, baking soda. In a large bowl, cream peanut butter, oil, and Xylosweet.

Beat in eggs one at a time, add vanilla and butter extracts.

Stir in oat mixture.

Spread in baking pan and bake 15-20min. (or until toothpick comes out clean). Allow brownies to cool; then cut into squares.

Nessey TIPS

Use almond butter or cashew butter instead of peanut butter for a fun variety.

For the **YF** version, substitute 3 cups almond flour instead of the oats

WEEK TWO

Did I Miss You?

Day 8

"But, Mom! I don't want to miss God!" It was Friday night, a muggy summer evening. I was sitting on my couch in my small apartment, dressed for bed, and had been on the phone for over an hour. My eyes were swollen, my face red and tear-stained from several hours of crying. I listened to my parents who, once again, cautiously and tenderly attempted to re-propose the unthinkable idea of me moving back home.

I had heard a distinct Word from the Lord to move from my home state of Texas with my pastor's family to the beautiful state of Tennessee. The Lord had miraculously opened so many doors for my transition to run relatively smoothly. Within my brief sojourn, I had held a job in an international ministry, began building a community of relationships spanning from downtown Nashville into the small quaint suburbs just south of the city. I was on a praise team, served as an administrative employee to help run conferences all over the area, looking at the prospect of some modeling and radio; I even lived in a beautiful apartment. However, by the time that everything seemed to be set, ready for me to plunge ahead full-throttle into the beginning of a new life, my health began to fail yet again ... and quickly.[1]

This phone conversation with my folks was one of the many that had begun to develop by the third month of my Tennessean experience. At the time of this transaction, I had already visited several specialized physicians, run a wide variety of tests in a number of hospitals and medical clinics, resigned my positions of employment and volunteer work, and had been "shut-up" in my apartment for several days, lacking the physical strength to leave for more than an hour at a time. Still, I knew that God had called me to *this place* for a reason! I *knew* I was supposed to be here until the Lord called me out! I was *not* going to give in! I would persevere!

"No! God called me *here*. I know He did! There's something for me to do *here*, but it hasn't happened yet. I've only been here four months ..." We exchanged a few more words, prayed, and hung up the phone. Although I boldly professed my faith to

> Most of us, at one time or another, come to this crossroads of belief, asking, "Can I even hear from God? Have I just completely lost it?"

persevere and "never give up" in my attempts to bat down my parents' caring notions with "spiritual reasoning," I knew deep down that my parents were speaking wisdom. I knew that, with the rapidity of my health's decline, it would be only a matter of weeks before I would be barely able to move home without suffering severe trauma to my already fragile physical state. I knew that I would need the caretaking of my family, who were familiar with my past health difficulties, and who could see my imminent relapse. I knew they were right; I knew that I probably did need to move home, and soon.

I buried my face in my hands ... I tried to cry, but no tears came; I was just too tired physically, emotionally, and spiritually. I was at a crossroads of belief. "Oh Lord. I don't get it ... was I wrong; did I just miss You?"

Did I Miss You?

Day 8
(continued)

Have you ever come to a place or situation in your life where you felt, in your gut, that you knew, without a shadow of a doubt, that you had heard a word from the Lord; you stepped out in faith, believing His guidance, and, despite all your prayers and supplication, your actions flopped? I think most of us, at one time or another, come to this crossroads of belief, that collision of faith and reason, asking, "Can I even *hear* from God? Have I just completely lost it?"

Jesus answers our queries by saying, *"My sheep hear My voice. And the voice of a stranger, they will not follow"* (Jn. 10:27, 5). I cannot tell you how many times I read that Scripture over and over and *over* when I began to weigh in the decision of staying in Tennessee or moving back home. I *knew* I had heard from God, and I had followed the path of His leading in blind faith, trusting Him to lead in me in the way everlasting ... but the way everlasting took an unexpected turn for the worse. Why did this path

> **Sometimes, trials emerge because we *are* walking in perfect obedience. Why? The Lord allows us to face adversity with Him in order to draw us into a closer reliance upon Him ...**

turn perilous? Was it because I was disobedient or in sin? Was I not walking in "enough faith" for my way to prosper the way *I* thought it should?

Before I go any further, I do need to point out that there are times when we do get "off track." There are times when we harbor an offense, or do or watch something that we know is not "100% right or wrong," but it is not something, which is pleasing to God or considered a "good witness" of our faith. In addition, and I am going to get in trouble for this one, there are the times when we "forget" to tithe, or do not believe in the Biblical principle. In circumstances such as these, our spiritual ears lose their keenness to hearing the voice of our Shepherd. That is why the Bible says, *"Confess your sins one to another,"* and, *"... first be reconciled with your brother, then bring an offering"* (Jms. 5:16; Matt. 5:24).

It is not for God's sake that we do this, but for ours! He so desperately *wants* us to hear Him, but when we start gradually walking away from the "straight and narrow," we lose our sensitivity to hear His voice. If anything, God's voice is muddled, and our discernment less clear when we are not right before Him. Therefore, the first course of action is *always* to come before the throne of grace and ask the Lord, as David did, to search our hearts to see if there be any false way within us (Ps.139:23-24). If so, we do need to repent so that our relationship with Him will no longer be estranged.

But, what if there *isn't* anything "blatantly" wrong? Not that we are ever "perfect," but what if we *have* been walking "right" before God, and He doesn't correct us when we ask Him? This is the pinnacle of faith, in which I "got stuck." I cried out to God, threw myself at the Mercy Seat of His Grace, "God if there be *anything* wrong in my heart, show me and I will confess! I'm ready; let me have it," and then I braced myself for His chastisement and conviction ... but none came. Yes, this was a relief at first, but then I grew puzzled and frustrated. "... um, well ... If

I'm not 'off', Lord, then ... why in the world did You lead me to *this*?! This is *not* what I had in mind when You called me here! I walked out in faith! I trusted You, and now *this*?!"

Sound familiar? Maybe you stepped out in faith, perhaps you gave an offering as the Lord led you, and then you had to foreclose on your house. Or, you may have ministered to a friend in need in faith that you were sowing seeds of righteousness and blessing him or her in the way that Christ would have done, only to be horrendously betrayed and taken advantage of. "But God! I trusted You! Why have You forsaken me?!" Whether we wish to or not, we have a tendency to place certain expectations on God when we follow Him in faith and act in obedience to His Word. We presume that "all will be well," and God will reward us for our faithful obedience. True, He will reward us for our obedience; but our reward does not come without a cost.

When God calls us to walk on a road that takes unexpected turns into trials, it isn't always because we are walking in disobedience. Sometimes, trials emerge *because* we are walking in perfect obedience. Why? The Lord allows us to face adversity *with* Him in order to draw us into a closer reliance *upon* Him, actually *strengthening* our faith in His guidance and sharpening our ability to hear His still small voice.

But what about our mistakes? We can be walking in His will, but that does not make us immune from walking without error. Sometimes, we make decisions that are rash, or we take out our frustration on someone else, only to have to go and clean up *that* mess in addition to the larger problem. I had to apologize several times to my parents when I took out my perplexity on them (you talk about humbling). This even led to additional anxiety, "Oh no. Now I *am* in sin; now I will miss God for sure! Oh, God help me! Remember that I am but dust ..." Then the

> Faith is the substance of things hoped for; a hope that is recognized in the peace shown in an individual's countenance; it is that inner rest that has this knowing that God is good and in control.

Lord led me to this verse in Psalms:

"*The steps of a man are established by the LORD, and He delights in his way. When he falls, he will not be hurled headlong (stumble), because the LORD is the One who holds his hand*" (Ps. 37: 23-24).

This passage suggests that for those who love the Lord and are making their best efforts to walk in His ways; their steps are *established* by Him. The Hebrew word for "established" in this passage is *Yeqamyâh*, which means, "Yahweh accomplishes; makes clear and good; causes to endure; holds, helps, and strengthens." Also, "delights" (Hebrew: *châphêts*) is "to be pleased with, to choose, to like someone or something very much."

In other words, when we do walk out in faith, the very steps we take are steps that *God* has made clear and good and on a path that *He* has not only chosen, but with which He is also *pleased*! Even when the path seems to turn for the worse, God has already

Did I Miss You?

Day 8 (continued)

ordained the "worse" as good. Isn't that incredible? We *can* believe that we hear the Lord even when our acts of faith and obedience do not always reap the kind of results we thought they should. Furthermore, if and when we do fall, make a mistake, "mess up," or "miss" Him on our walk of faith, we *will not stumble* because He holds us up with His right hand! Because He is our Shepherd, we never have to fear any evil, for He is with us! Now that is a comforting thought.

This kind of realization has not come easily for me. In fact, even now, I speak it *in faith* because this path, on which I have walked, quite frankly, has not made much sense to any cognitive reasoning or understanding of faith. To the practical sense, it seems as though I moved to Tennessee just to get sick again and be brought home; sheesh, what kind of a faith is that?! Well, one that believes that God is working all things together for the good of them, who love Him and have been called according to His purpose. No, I really do not know why God called me to Tennessee, although I do have some wonderful memories of my sojourn there. Furthermore, I do not know why He allowed me to relapse in my illness; but I learned more about His nature in the midst of my suffering because of it.

Faith is *not* the substance of things that go our way. It is *not* evidenced by all of our dreams coming true, or life being full of ease and always making perfect sense. Rather, faith is the substance of things *hoped* for; a hope that is recognized in the peace shown in an individual's countenance; it is that inner rest that has this "knowing" that God is *good* and in control. We do not miss God when we are doing our best to serve Him. We may make mistakes along the way, but we will not "miss" His path for our lives. They are *His* paths, and He loves His ways that He has set out for us. If He is the One Who holds them and causes them to endure, then our roads to righteousness will never fail, even when we do. God is faithful to keep us on track and hold us up with His mighty right hand. That is what His Word says, and His Word is true and everlasting ... His Word will not fail because *He will not fail*.

Did I "miss" God? Perhaps I made some mistakes along the way. Perhaps, in my attempts to serve Him, I fouled up from time to time. But, did I "miss" Him? Let us look at this in the reverse: God never "missed" me. We can trust that, when God is in control, He will make our paths straight. He is faithful to hold us, guide us, and walk us through our lives, especially when they do not make human sense. These are *His* paths of righteousness that He has designed for us to walk; and with them, He is well pleased, even when we are not. No, the path of righteousness will not always make sense to *our* expectations; but it will *always* make sense to His.

"The steps of a man are established by the LORD, and He delights in his way. When he falls, he will not be hurled headlong, because the LORD is the One who holds his hand."

Nessey's Nuts: Sugar 'N' Spice

Nessey's Sugar 'N Spice Nuts | YK

- **1** Egg White
- **5 c.** Mixed Nuts *(raw)*
- **1 tsp.** Water
- **1 c.** Xylosweet
- Coconut Oil *(for greasing pan)*
- **1 rounded tsp.** Ground Cinnamon
- **1 rounded tsp.** Ground Allspice
- **1 rounded tsp.** Ground Ginger
- **1 rounded tsp.** Ground Cloves
- **1 rounded tsp.** Ground Nutmeg

Preheat oven to 325° F. Grease 15"x10"x1" baking pan.

In large bowl, beat egg white and water until frothy.

Add nuts; toss to coat.

Combine Xylosweet and spices. Sprinkle mixture on nuts; toss to coat. Spread nuts in single layer in prepared pan.

Bake 20-22 minutes. Cool 10 minutes. Transfer to aluminum foil* to cool and harden (about 4 hrs).

Break into clusters.

Nessey TIPS

*I use aluminum foil to cool my nut mixes because other papers, such as wax paper and papers towels, will stick to the nuts. I noticed also that the nut mixes dry/cool a lot faster when on the aluminum foil.

Also try the exotic spices such as McCormick's Roasted Saigon Cinnamon, Chinese Ginger, etc. for more "expressive" tastes.

Gift of Faith

Day 9

Have you ever wondered why your problems never seem to go away? Have you ever been told or have wondered yourself, "It's because you lack faith." After all, I'm sure you have heard the Scripture, "If you have faith as small as a mustard seed, you can say to this mountain, 'Move from here to there,' and it will move"(Matt. 17:20). So, what happens when the mountain doesn't seem to move? You've prayed and pleaded and prayed some more for God to move your problem, to intervene in your circumstance ... and still nothing's happening.

Don't be discouraged. It's not that you lack faith. Perhaps, the Lord is actually *increasing* your faith as He takes you *through* this dark place.

I had a problem. I had an illness without any diagnosis, without any treatment, without any relief. I had faith! Every day, I prayed boldly to God for answers, and, bless God, He was going to answer my prayer! However, after years of *not* having Him answer my prayers the way *I* would have liked, I came to a realization that He just might have had a purpose in the suffering.

The Lord had chosen to develop in me, even more so, the gift of faith. Many years ago, at the beginning stages of my health problems, I felt strongly and prophesied boldly that I would be healed, by the power of the name of Jesus. I fearlessly professed how by His stripes, I was healed, and at the name of Jesus, every knee, every ailment and disease, must bow at His feet and that I was more than a conqueror in Christ Jesus, and so on. However, the illness continued and the symptoms worsened. Even so, I drew closer in relationship with the Father. He taught me that *healing* is not evidence of faith. In fact, sometimes it requires more faith to *rest* in the difficult circumstances than to be delivered *from* them. Time and again, I was thrust into the furnace of affliction, and with every passing day that the ailment remained, I increasingly understood in deeper levels of revelation that, even though the Lord was leaving this thorn, I could still trust that His purposes for my life would be fulfilled despite the malady. Verses such as, "No weapon formed against (me) shall prosper" (Isa. 54:17), took on new meaning. Weapons may form and they may last, but they will not prosper in hindering the promises of God from coming to fruition in our lives. As He walked me through that valley, I learned new depths of fearing no evil. As He burned His nature into my spirit through suffering, His light began to radiate in even greater ways in every area of my life. Though He slay me, yet I trusted Him.

It's not that we don't have faith when we continue to face our dilemmas. On the contrary, it may very well be that we are considered by God among those with GREAT faith. As difficult as it may be to remain in the troubling circumstance, we can, by His grace, rejoice and be glad! God has not forgotten us! In fact, He is far closer to us than He could have been had He removed our crises. For the Lord is close to the brokenhearted and He will not forsake the afflicted ones (Isa. 57:15, 41:17). We *can* trust, lean on, and rely on our Shepherd (Prov. 3:5). And, in so doing, we will learn the kindness and gentleness of His ways as He walks us *through* the valley of our darkest shadows (ref. Matt. 11:29, Ps. 23:4).

Nessey's Nuts: Texas Spice

YK

2 c. (rounded)	Mixed Nuts (raw)
1 Tbsp.	Safflower Oil
1 Tbsp.	*Sweet N' Natural®
1 tsp.	Sea Salt
1/2 tsp.	Ground Garlic Granules
1/2 tsp.	Ground Cumin
1/4 tsp.	Cayenne Pepper
3 to 4 c.	Water (see Nessey Tip)

*Sweet N' Natural is an erythritol sweetener. You can purchase it at Physician's Preference (www.physicianspreference.com)

Preheat oven to 400° F.

In a pot, bring water to a boil. Dump nuts into water and turn off stove. Let sit for 2 min. Drain nuts in spaghetti strainer, then pour onto baking sheet. Place in oven and toast for 10-15 min. (or until lightly browned).

Mix spices in small bowl and set aside. In a skillet, heat oil on medium, then pour toasted nuts into skillet and toss nuts (with spatula) for 1 minute (make sure nuts are well coated with oil). Turn off stove and pour spices onto nuts, then continue to toss nuts with spatula until nuts are well-coated. Transfer to aluminum foil to completely cool.

Nessey TIPS

I am generous with my measurements on the spices, adds more flavor that way.

It's always best to use some type of distilled water to boil the nuts: the flavor is much cleaner, and you won't have to worry about chemicals in the water.

Also, you want the nuts to be "smoking" while you're tossing them in the skillet—it gives them a robust yummy flavor. DO NOT double the recipe! It will not turn out well. Just repeat for more mix. These nuts store well for weeks to months. Make sure they are completely cool before storing or they will lose their crispyness.

Faith to Wait in the Storm

Day 10

And immediately, He made the disciples get into the boat, and go ahead of Him to the other side. (Matt. 14:22)

It was the end of a wonderful day. The Master had just performed an amazing miracle, creating a feast for a multitude from a few morsels of a boy's lunch. Imagine, watching the Teacher, taking the bread (as He always did) blessing it, breaking it, and passing it to His disciples to give to the people ... but this time, He kept breaking it, and breaking it, and breaking it, and it continued to multiply until everyone present was fed and satisfied! What a glorious day! Talk about a spiritual high! Those disciples must have felt so "close to God," especially after witnessing *and participating* in such an incredible event. And they were this Man's CLOSE companions! They were His "right hand guys"! Now, the sun was setting, the crowds were leaving, and so, it was time for a new task – the Master said, "Go to the other side of the lake; I'll catch up with you." No problem!

Or so they thought ... but as night fell, and the boat went further and further away from the shore, a storm emerged; the winds raged "against them" (vs.24) ... and the Master was nowhere in sight ...

We all enjoy those spiritual highs, don't we? You remember that glorious feeling inside right after the conference? Summer camp? The church retreat? Or right after you were baptized? Oh! The world was such a beautiful place! Life was everywhere! God was in everything! The sun shone brighter; the colors of the trees and sky were more brilliant; everything seemed so fresh and clean! From now on, life was going to be different! You had just been in the presence of Jesus, and He had changed your life! You and He are *unstoppable*! What can the enemy throw at you that you and God can't handle?! And when He asks you to take another step of faith, you gladly accept His request and quickly obey! After all, He only has good in mind for you, right?

So you step out in obedience, and suddenly ... storms. You leave your old job, but the new company *doesn't* hire you, and your bills start to pile higher and higher. You place membership at the new church, but no one speaks to you. You ask the elders to pray over your illness, but your condition continues to decline. You seek counseling for your marriage, but your spouse insists on a divorce. You release your rebelling teen to the Lord, but his behavior goes from bad to worse.

What do you do when you obey God in full faith, and instead of things getting better, they get worse? What happened?! You were so close to God! You just had a wonderful experience with Him! Everything was going to be different! He told you to step out in faith and expect Him to intervene in your situation, and so you do ... and life's messes become nightmarish! "Did I hear God right? Was I supposed to do this? What am I going to do? They're going to turn off my electricity? Travis was arrested! The

doctor says I have 3 months to live!!!"

Is this fair? Is this right? Your obedience "rewarded" with the "winds of life" turning against you? This is what the disciples were thinking when they were in the middle of the lake. They had just witnessed one of Christ's most famous miracles, and actually participated in it, having been asked to distribute the miraculous food to the masses *and* pick up the leftovers. They were on "Cloud 9;" nothing could stop them now! And Jesus told them to cross the lake and He would catch up with them, no problem! "But wait a minute! He didn't tell us about the storm? He didn't tell us that the winds would be so harsh, the waves would climb so high, the thunder would boom so loud! Did we hear Him right? Did He want us to cross the lake? We're not going to make it! This storm is too strong!!!"

No, Jesus didn't tell them about the storm; He *did* tell them to "cross the lake." That was all they needed to know ... and guess what? He did what He promised. He "caught up with them," and they crossed to the other side.

"And in the fourth watch of the night, He came to them, walking on the sea ... and when (He) got into the boat, the wind stopped ... and when they had crossed over, they came to the land ..." (vs. 25, 32, 34).

When we step out in faith and obedience, we are not always ensured that we are going to have "smooth sailing" in the beginning. In fact, it is arguable to say that, more often times than not, we *are* going to experience "contrary winds" in our circumstances initially. Leaving one job to go to another requires a lot of transitions in finances, time, and effort; joining a new church means that you have to exert extra effort to "get plugged in." And don't forget the spiritual aspect of it:

"For our struggle is not against flesh and blood ... but against the spiritual forces of wickedness in the heavenly places" (Eph. 6:12).

Do you think the enemy is going to stand idly by and *let* you gain more ground of his territory? Absolutely not! If God wants you in this new church fellowship, the enemy will attempt to make it clear that you "don't belong." If the Lord wants to heal your body, the enemy will do everything he can to get you to believe He doesn't. If God wants to deliver your son from his wayward life, the enemy will do everything possible to thwart His plans of deliverance by tempting you to act out in your emotions and not in obedience. We mustn't forget that we have an enemy, whose plan is to destroy our faith and our relationship with the Father.

God is faithful. What He says He will do, He will do; what He says will happen, will happen. Jesus told His disciples to cross the lake, and though a storm emerged, His disciples *did* cross that lake. Whatever it is the Lord has promised you, He will do it. The storm may be raging, the winds may be contrary, but know that Christ will come and meet you, like He said He would.

You had the faith to get in the boat *to* cross the lake; do you have the faith to wait in the storm until you do?

> The storm may be raging, the winds may be contrary, but know that Christ will come and meet you, like He said He would.

"Sugar" Cookies

"Sugar" Cookies | YK

Nessey TIPS

1/4 c.	Coconut Oil
3/4 c.	Xylosweet
1	Egg
1 Tbsp.	Unsweetened Almond Milk
3-1/4 c.	Almond Flour
1/8 tsp.	Salt
1/4 tsp.	Baking Soda
1/2 tsp.	Vanilla Extract
1/2 tsp.	Butter Extract

Preheat oven to 350° F.

Cream oil, eggs, Xylosweet, and flavorings. Add almond milk.

In another bowl, mix flour, salt, baking powder. Add dry blend to wet and mix well.

Drop by spoonfuls on baking sheet; bake for 10 min. Remove from oven and allow to cool on baking sheet for a few minutes (this way the cookies are moist).

For Snickerdoodle Cookies, add 1/4 tsp. of cinnamon, nutmeg, and cloves to dry mix, then sprinkle cookies with cinnamon before baking.

For Butter Cookies, use butter in place of coconut oil (**YF**).

Disappointed Hope

Day 11

Those who hope in Me will never be disappointed.

(Isa. 49:23)

Such a wonderful promise: when we trust God and wait for Him, we will never be disappointed! For the believer, this is superb news! Never a disappointment?! How can any Christian be anything *but* incredulously exuberant with such a promise like that!

But, as you and I know all too well ... this doesn't always seem to be the case, does it? What human being has never EVER been disappointed? What about those times when, you're in a money crunch, but you're believing God to work all things out for good, and you have a meeting with your boss. Excited, nervous, but "full of faith," you walk into that office and think, "Well Lord, this is it. You know I've been believing You to work out my money dilemma. Maybe I'll be getting a raise, or he'll give me a bonus, or something. Grant me favor with my boss today." Your boss has you sit in the chair opposite his desk. As you look at his expression, you immediately realize that this is not the face of a generous promoter, but one of grave crisis intervention. Grim, eyes downcast, he thumbs through what appears to be your file, which he closes, lays resolutely on his desk, and slowly lifts his eyes, looking at you for the first time, and methodically begins the sad monologue of the economic crisis, its affect on the company, the forced layoffs of employees, and how your work, though commendable and an asset to the organization, was no longer needed. With file in hand, you stagger your way out of the office, down the hall, making your way to your car, shocked, perplexed, all the while screaming in your heart, "Lord! Why have You forsaken me?!"

> You call up your prayer warriors, send in prayer requests to churches all over town, fasts are initiated, offerings are made in faith for a miracle breakthrough ... the condition worsens and finally, the prognosis proves true, and you lay your beloved to rest in a pillowed coffin.

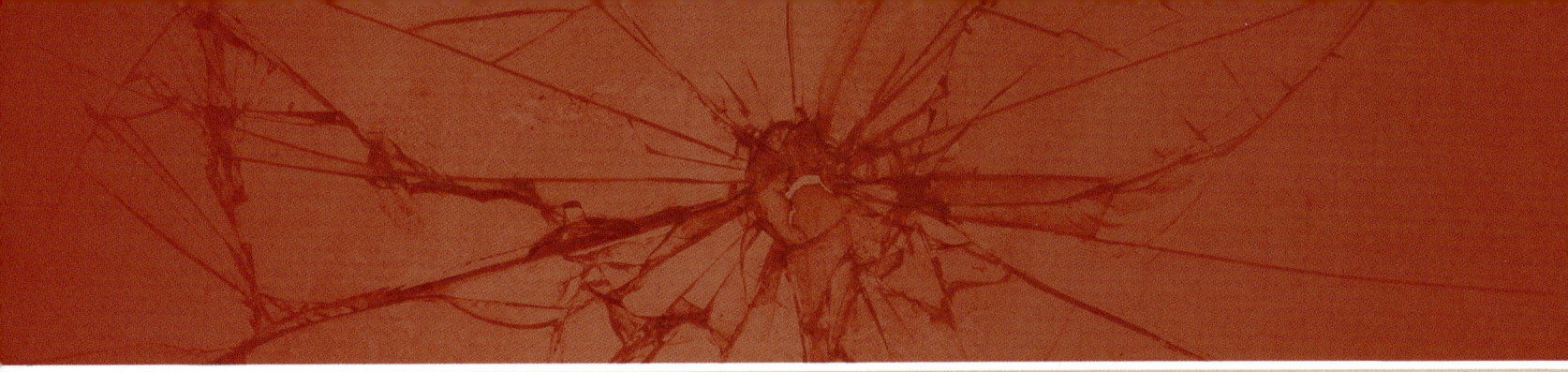

What about the times when you are believing God for the healing for a loved one? The prognosis is grim, the doctors give little hope for recovery, but you believe in a God, Who makes all things possible! You call up your prayer warriors, send in prayer requests to churches all over town, fasts are initiated, offerings are made in faith for a miracle breakthrough … and the condition worsens and finally, the prognosis proves true, and you lay your beloved to rest in a pillowed coffin. Anger rent with unutterable sorrow wells inside your heart as you ride in the limousine, exiting the cemetery. Your mind is spinning, battered back and forth, like an ocean bobber caught in a hurricane, with a torrent of thoughts, memories, Scriptures, sermons, jostling in your head. Clenching your jaw, vainly attempting to hold back the wave of tears, you cry out, "My God! Why have You forsaken me?!"

Yes, you and I have all experienced extreme disappointments during our lives. Even when we are trusting God to come through, intervene, do the impossible, yet, for reasons we may never know in this life, He says, "No." So how can it be that those who hope in Him are never disappointed? Is this verse false?

There have been countless times, in which I have prayed and believed God to intervene in numerous difficult situations, in my own life as well as others', only to be denied my requests and left downcast in bitter disappointment. One time specifically, after my perception of the "worst case scenario" came true, I shut myself in my room, sat angrily at my desk, ripped open my Bible to the above Scripture, and with tears of anger and confusion streaming down my face, defiantly pointed to the verse and told the Lord through sobs, "You said I would NOT be disappointed if I hoped in You! But Lord! That is EXACTLY what I am feeling right now!"

It was then that He revealed to me to root of my disappointment. My hope was not in *Him*; it was in the result I wanted *from* Him. I was hoping that God would answer me the way that seemed best to me, and when He did not, my emotions were shattered and my exasperation with Him paramount. The depth of my emotion only revealed the extent, in which I had placed my hope in something *other* than the Lord.

> It was then that He revealed to me to root of my disappointment. My hope was not in Him; it was in the result I wanted from Him.

But this is not God's best for us: our emotions jolting up and down, peaks and valleys, as we hope and pray for His will to be done in our lives. This is not the faith, to which we are called. The faith that God intends for us to have is a steady, peaceful trust, knowing that, whatever the outcome, it is <u>His</u> best and <u>He</u> <u>will</u> work it out for our good. It is a resting place, secure in His character and in His goodness, not placing parameters on how He can answer us in order for us to "feel" happy with His will and with our faith. God doesn't ask us for our opinion about His answers; He only asks us to believe in Him, no matter *how* He answers.

Consider a scenario: how many people prayed that night Jesus went to trial, praying that God

Disappointed Hope

Day 11

would rescue this Good Teacher from the hands of the Pharisees and Romans? And did He? No. The Lord allowed His Son to die on the cross, crucified, a horrific torturous death, condemned by preposterous allegations. The worst possible outcome to the situation came true. But would you, 21st century believer, have wanted God to have answered those

> The Word of God is true. If our hope is in Him, we will never be disappointed.

heartfelt prayers of Christ's first century followers any other way? Of course not! Without the death of Christ, there would have been no resurrection of Jesus Christ, no hope of eternal glory or promise of everlasting life. You would not know what true joy and peace are; there would be no assurance of being loved by God, or anyone for that matter; there would be no purpose or reason to live. Life would be utterly meaningless! It was *because* Christ died that we enjoy these blessings! But how could those, who were interceding on Jesus's behalf that night, ever have imagined this glorious result, which would come as a consequence of the Lord's refusal of their requests?! They couldn't have because the Lord initiated a new era! God's ultimate answer to these prayer requests far surpassed what any human being could have EVER contemplated at that time!

If God can completely change the world with a refusal *then*, He most certainly can cause similar results with His denials to us *now*. We may not be able to know or understand the thoughts of our Father when He answers us in ways that seem so wrong in light of our desires. And we may be disappointed with the initial outcome; but if we hope in Him, He will turn the situation around for a good that is far more inconceivably glorious than we could have EVER begun to fathom or imagine, causing an end that would have been thwarted if God answered us "our way."

The Word of God is true. If our hope is in Him, we will never be disappointed. And when those feelings of disappointment rise, and your emotions become fractured, take heart. God will not disappoint you when He completes His purpose in your situation. Though the initial answer may, His end will not. God is able to do exceedingly, abundantly, above all that we could ever dare to hope, ask, or think. In the end, you will be overwhelmingly grateful that He answered in the way that He did.

Soft Peanut Butter Cookies

YK

- **1 c.** Xylosweet
- **1 c.** Unsweetened Creamy Peanut Butter
- **1** Egg
- **1 tsp.** Vanilla

Preheat oven to 325° F.

Mix ingredients with spoon until just blended.

Drop in spoonfuls on baking sheet. Take a fork and crisscross each cookie.

Bake for 10 – 11 min. Allow to cool on baking sheet, then serve.

Nessey TIPS

These cookies are supposed to finish cooking while they are cooling! Make sure you take them out at 10 minutes and let them completely cool on the baking sheet (that's what makes them soft and gooey).

Suffering for Righteousness

Day 12

"But even if you should suffer for the sake of righteousness, you are blessed" (1 Pet. 3:14).

What does it mean to suffer for righteousness's sake? What all does that include? Does that only infer enduring persecution for your faith? Walking through the barrage of insults thrown at you from jealous peers, who despise your "holiness" trek? Or is this talking about the more severe persecution: the literal physical beatings, imprisonment, even execution for your faith in Jesus Christ?

Yes, it can mean all of these things. Suffering for righteousness is typically thought of in that light ... but I believe there's more to this phrase than this initial interpretation ...

Righteousness – what is that? God called Abraham righteous because "he believed God."[1] That's it! That's all that righteousness really is ... it is believing God. Notice, I did not say, "believe *in* God" or "believe *there is* a God." There's a difference: for even the demons believe that there is a God and shudder.[2] No: it's believe God ... only believe, as Jesus says.[3] So – that seems pretty simple, doesn't it ... *too* simple in fact. What's in this "believing" business? Surely there's a catch, right?

Yes! But it's not what you think ... believing God, simply and only believing Him means ... trust. Ouch. Now THAT'S a little word that carries a lot of punch, isn't it? This little word, that looks so harmless on paper, demands something from us. It means that no matter what happens, no matter what hardships, heartbreaks, or disappointments we face, we continue to remain steadfast in our belief in God's love for us, that He has not changed His mind toward us, that no matter what happens, no matter WHAT happens ... He still loves us ...

Trust God, believe God, this is righteousness.

So, back to the initial question, what does it mean to suffer for righteousness's sake? Well, this suffering comes in a variety of ways: persecution, sure ... but what about the times when life just keeps falling apart? Your wife walks out the door? You find that pink slip on your desk? Your pastor confesses adultery from the pulpit? Your daughter calls from prison? These are the times when trusting God seems ludicrous. Why continue to trust when He, apparently, lets you down? This, dear friend, is suffering for righteousness ...

Trusting God despite all reason and circumstance is never easy. In fact, it can be utterly excruciating and exhausting! It HURTS to continue to trust when everything in you SCREAMS to let it go and forget it. "Why don't you just curse God and die" as Job's wife says.[4] It is sheer AGONY to hang onto faith when your circumstances SHRIEK of God's displeasure or disdain for you ... it would seem only natural to follow Job's wife's suggestion, right?

It may be natural, but we are called to the *super*natural. We are called to stretch beyond the surface and cling to the deeper things, the spiritual things, the righteous things. And we, being mortal, cannot do this on our own: we need His Spirit.

We are never alone in our pursuit of righteousness. We have a Helper to carry us through those times when we so desire to throw away everything we've ever believed. Our Keeper keeps us when we can't keep ourselves. He holds our hands tight around our grasp of faith, even though our hands may weaken in their grip. He's the One, who sustains us in trust: *He* keeps us in righteousness.

Rejoice, beloved! Though you suffer through life's trials and tribulations, hold onto faith! For your faith is righteousness, and if you suffer for its sake, you are BLESSED!

Nessey's Nutty Cookies

YF

1/2 c.	Butter	
1 c.	Xylosweet	
1	Egg	
	or	
2	Egg Whites	
1/2 c.	Unsweetened Peanut Butter	
1/2 tsp.	Vanilla	
1-1/2 c.	Almond Flour (Bob's Red Mill)	
1 c.	Flaxseed Meal (Bob's Red Mill)	
3/4 tsp.	Baking Powder	
1/4 tsp.	Baking Soda	
1/2 c.	Chopped Peanuts (optional)	

Preheat oven to 350° F.

Mix melted butter with Xylosweet. Add egg; mix well. Stir in peanut butter and vanilla; beat until smooth.

Blend rest of dry ingredients together. Add dry to wet mixture and mix well.

Drop by teaspoons onto ungreased cookie sheet. Criss-cross on each cookie with fork tines.

Bake about 10 min., then remove and allow to cool on baking sheet before removing them (makes them chewy).

Makes 36-40 cookies.

Nessey TIPS

Sometimes for extra crunch I use 1/3 c. of chopped peanuts.

Optional **Y2F** Variation: Replace Almond Flour with 1-1/2 c. Oat Flour. (Arrowhead Mills)

The Coffin

Day 13

Death has been swallowed up in victory.

(1Cor 15:54)

Trapped. You know the feeling. It's a suffocating place. Though the sun may be shining outside, you feel the dark all around you. It's not visible, but it's very real. It's as if the walls around you are caving in, whether you're inside or out in an open field. You can't escape the feeling. You tell yourself that it IS just a feeling, right? There's no reason for the emotional panic that is threatening to clench your throat. You're ok. You'll be fine. The sun is bright, the wind is fresh, the day is young ... but still ... you just can't seem to shake it ... that feeling ... trapped.

What I've described is a desperate place, a dire place, a horrid place that none of us ever wish to come to; but we do. It happens in the times when everything in our life is out of control, caving in around us, going wrong, and there's NOTHING we can do about it. Your job is a dead end; your kids insist on their rebellion; your husband refuses to meet you halfway; your illness grows steadily worse despite everything you do. There's no escaping the seemingly inevitable. You are trapped in a sinking pool of hardship and there's no way out.

You're right. There *is* no way out ... it's *through*. Trials come, and they linger, and our society tries to engrave in our brains that we can escape their discomfort. But in all honesty, we can't escape them. In fact, we may not really want to, if we knew the consequences of going through. Through gets us to the

> Through gets us to the other side, stronger and wiser. It's through the fire that gold is made brighter. It's through the cocoon that the butterfly's wings are enabled to carry its weight in flight.

other side, stronger, wiser. It's through the fire that gold is made brighter. It's through the cocoon that the butterfly's wings are enabled to carry its weight in flight. Did you know that a chick will die if it is not forced to peck its way through the shell that encases it at hatching time? Did you know that silver

would have little to no value if it was not heated to an intolerable temperature that carries its impurities out of its matter?

What scares us about the "through" part of hardship is what causes the trapped feeling: it's the coffin. Yes, the coffins in life are the places where we utterly die to our old lives and become something new. The caterpillar dies in the coffin of the cocoon and is liquefied during the metamorphic process. The hard stone and metal die from their previous forms in the fire, completely dissolved in the heat. The egg yolk and shell die as the tiny little bird completely engulfs them as it grows within the egg.

Before new life, before resurrection, death must happen. Jesus knew this. Oh the trapped feeling He must have felt, crying out in utter despair to His Father the night before His crucifixion, "Father if You are willing!"[1] His face dampened by His sweat, His forehead stained with His blood bursting through His pores. He was trapped. There was no way out. There was just ... through.

But without that through, you and I would have no hope. Without His through, you and I would have no peace. Without His through, you and I would be lost to our coffins. There would be no other side to them: there would be no life after death, literal or metaphorical; no joy after sorrow, or reward after loss. Christ went through His "through," and as a result, He reigns over all things and has seated us with Him over all things.[2] As a result, we can look at our coffins as places of opportunity, as the place of strength and fulfillment of our ultimate purposes; the place where you and I become all we were created and meant to be, rather than the pit of hellacious despair and sheer horror. We can go *through* our coffins because Christ went through His.

We can go *through* our coffins because Christ went through His.

Whatever trapped place you may find yourself in right now, whatever coffin stands in your way at this moment; don't try to get out of it. Because of Jesus, you *can* go through it; and trust me, there is life on the other side. The egg gives way to the chick; the rock and ore give way to the gold, the cocoon gives way to the butterfly; and your coffin gives way to the you God intended for you to become. Press on, and press *through*.

"Therefore, my dear brothers, stand firm. Let nothing move you. Always give yourselves fully to the work of the Lord, because you know that your labor in the Lord is not in vain" (1Cor 15:58).

Christmas Cookies

Christmas Cookies | Y2F

1/4 c.	Coconut Oil
3/4 c.	Xylosweet
1	Egg
1 Tbsp.	Unsweetened Almond Milk
1-1/4 c.	Oat Flour
1/8 tsp.	Salt
1/4 tsp.	Baking Soda
1/4 tsp.	Ground Cinnamon
1/4 tsp.	Ground Allspice
1/4 tsp.	Ground Ginger
1/4 tsp.	Ground Cloves
1/4 tsp.	Ground Nutmeg
Aside:	*Small Cup of Cinnamon and Xylosweet, Mixed*

Preheat oven to 350° F.

Cream oil, eggs, Xylosweet. Add almond milk.

In another bowl, mix oat flour, salt, baking powder, and spices. Add dry blend to the wet and mix well.

Drop spoonfuls of dough onto baking sheet. In a small cup mix additional cinnamon and Xylosweet then sprinkle each cookie with Xylosweet/cinnamon mix.

Bake for 10 min.-12 min., then remove from oven and allow to cool on baking sheet.

Nessey TIPS

What is Christmas without Hot Cocoa? Check out this recipe (borrowed from my friends at Hotze Health & Wellness Center) as an excellent accompaniment to go with your cookies!

Hot Cocoa (YK)
1-1/2 c. Unsweetened Chocolate Almond Milk (Blue Diamond "Almond Breeze" – see Brands)
1 Tbsp. Unsweet Cocoa Powder
2 Tbsp. Xylosweet

Blend all ingredients until smooth. Warm in skillet or microwave to desired temperature and SERVE!

Variations: add **1/8 tsp.** of Hazelnut, Vanilla, or other extract for additional flavors.

Immovable Mountains

Day 14

"So, what if the mountain *doesn't* move?" I'm sure you've heard the popular and quite powerful message that you can have the faith even as small as a mustard seed and be able to "move mountains." And if you think about it, that is one of the most encouraging and inspiring messages of faith in the whole of Scripture! After all, the mustard seed is the smallest seed; and what Jesus was saying was that you can have just a tiny speck of faith – shaky, barely felt, but there; an itty bitty faith in God's ability to change your circumstances and bring you out victoriously – to speak to your problem and BOOM! The mountain will move!

> He can take your little seed of faith and use it on your mountain of troubles, completely transforming the most perplexing situation into a citadel of triumph!

Say you have a crisis – you were laid off at work, your rent is overdue, and you just received a letter from the electric company that your electricity will be cut off if your bill is not paid by noon that Friday. Talk about a mountain of trouble! Despite the cataclysmic essence of these circumstances, you still barely hold on to the Lord's promises that, if you believe in Him and His ability to deliver you, even if your faith *isn't* very strong because you are overwhelmed by your situation, nevertheless, you can still speak to that mountain, "God, I trust You in this issue! I can't meet my financial needs, but I speak in faith that You will deliver me, somehow. Help me to trust in You ..." And suddenly, an answer comes! You get a phone call from a friend, who felt the Lord leading them to give you a certain amount of money, which happens to be the *exact* amount of your rent. Then, the electric company calls, apologizing for the notice they sent you, finding that you had a credit on your account, so you won't be billed for the next two months! And *then*, the phone rings a *third* time, and it's a human resources agent from a local business office, who just received your resume and a positive referral and would like to interview you for a possible job! BOOM! The mountain moves!

This is how quickly God can work! He can take your little seed of faith in His "bigness" and use it on your mountain of troubles, completely transforming the most perplexing situation into a citadel of triumph! Suddenly!

But, as we all well know, though this kind of turnaround is not impossible and does occur from time to time, it doesn't always work that way, does it? Sometimes, even with the faith of the Biblical mustard *tree*, which is the largest tree there is, the mountain still DOES NOT MOVE. You pray fervently and confidently, "God, I trust in You! You can deliver me from this mess! I speak to this situation and say that You will be glorified in my crisis! You have all power and authority and I release it onto my circumstances," ... but ... they still cut off your lights; you go weeks without work; you find yourself getting deeper and deeper in debt, trying to stay in your home and paying rent with loans ... what then? How do you reconcile Christ's promise and inspirational principle on faith and declaration when your life experience seems to prove otherwise?

This second scenario seems to happen more often than not. Oh, we *love* to hear the stories and testimonies of the first. We shout and "hallelujah" the sermons and teachings on the promise of deliverance, "All you need is faith! It's faith that moves mountains." But sometimes, our deliverance *doesn't* come, at least, not the way we'd have hoped it would. We begin to question ourselves, "Is it because I don't have enough faith? Did I not declare it 'right'? Is there hidden sin in my heart? Why is this still happening to me? Why does the mountain not move?" Though we should seek our hearts and check our spirits for doubt, sin, and unbelief, we must also recognize that sometimes, the mountains don't move, not because of lack of faith, but because of God's greater purposes.

"O LORD, by Your **favor**, You have made my mountain to stand strong" (Ps. 30:7).

What in the world is the psalmist saying here?! God's *favor* makes the mountain to stand strong?! Yes. Out of His love for us, God will KEEP the

> God will KEEP the mountain right where it is ... because He loves you!

mountain right where it is, let you persevere through the storm and crisis, let you face the "worst case scenario." Why? Because He loves you! This is not always what we like to hear. We want to hear ways of "getting out" of our crises, escape our ailments, be rescued away from all our fears. But God and life don't always work that way. Moreover, what is even *more* perplexing about this verse is the fact that God won't let your mountain move *because of* His favor (i.e. His overabundant LOVE) for you!

"If God loved me, then why would He let this happen to me?" Martha and Mary asked the same question. They sent for Jesus when their brother, Jesus's dear friend, was sick. And guess what? Jesus *didn't* come. He stayed right where He was and let their mountain remain. And to add insult to injury, the Bible says He did this because He "loved" them (Jn. 11: 5-6). Excuse me? He *loved* this family, so He *let* them suffer and confront their worst fears? How is THAT love?!

Thankfully, Jesus explains, "*This sickness* (mountain) *is ... for the glory of God, so that the Son of God may be glorified by it*" (Jn. 11:4). In other words, the mountain Martha, Mary, and Lazarus were facing was going to remain because Christ was going to glorify Himself *through* their mountain, and then allow them to participate in His triumph!

We all know the story: Jesus raises Lazarus from the dead. But have you ever read the following verses and the next chapter *after* this great miracle?

Time and again, the Scriptures state that because of *Lazarus* people were coming from all over the region to see this resurrected man and the One, who raised him, and consequently, a "**multitude**" believed in Christ's divinity! They weren't just coming to see Jesus! They wanted to see LAZARUS! Lazarus became the celebrated vessel of Christ's glory!

Had Jesus moved the mountain beforehand, Martha, Mary, and Lazarus would have missed out on being Christ's most effective evangelistic tools in the final days of His earthly ministry! Oh, there would have been "shouts" and "hallelujahs" over Lazarus's healing, but the extent of his ministry

Immovable Mountains

Day 14

would have ended that day and been limited to a small group of witnesses. God didn't want this family, whom He loved dearly, to be limited in their influence – He wanted them to experience a grander scope of His glory and be powerful tools of ministry

> Had Jesus moved the mountain beforehand, Martha, Mary, and Lazarus would have missed out on being Christ's most effective evangelistic tools in the final days of His earthly ministry!

that even had the religious authorities trembling![1] It was His **FAVOR** that propelled them into this new dimension of triumph and effectiveness!

But what had to come first? An immovable mountain that WOULD NOT budge, even with all the faith they could muster. And yes, they had to go *through* their worst fears.

If you are in a crisis, and you have been praying, asking, pleading with God to move the mountain of adversity, and your mountain still isn't moving, take heart. It's not that God doesn't hear you; He does. It's not that you don't have enough faith; you do. Maybe this mountain is not supposed to be moved like you'd like. Perhaps this mountain is not necessarily an obstacle *against* you, but a gift of God's favor *for* you! What if this mountain is actually saying how much God loves you, and reveals His insatiable desire for you to experience a side of His glory that will catapult you into a realm of ministerial influence that you couldn't have possibly imagined? What if He plans to share a triumph with you that is so incredible and glorious that many people will believe in Him all because they saw *you*?! This mountain isn't an indictment on your faith; it's a sign of your preciousness to the Father!

Don't despair. Your mountain may remain for a little while, but your certain victory will make all the tears, all the perplexity, and all the heartache you endured in your crisis more than worth the while.

"This sickness is not to end in death, but for the glory of God, so that the Son of God may be glorified by it."

"Tea Time" Spice Cakes

"Tea Time" Spice Cakes | YK

Nessey TIPS

1 c.	Coconut Oil
3/4 c.	Xylosweet
4	Eggs
4 Tbsp.	Unsweetened Almond Milk
1-1/4 c.	Coconut Flour *(sifted)*
1/8 tsp.	Salt
1/4 tsp.	Baking Soda
1/4 tsp.	Ground Cinnamon
1/4 tsp.	Nutmeg
1/4 tsp.	Ginger
1/4 tsp.	Allspice
1/4 tsp.	Cloves
Aside:	*Small Cup of Cinnamon and Xylosweet, Mixed*

Preheat oven to 350° F.

Cream oil, eggs and Xylosweet. Add almond milk.

In another bowl, mix coconut flour, salt, baking powder, and spices (except the cinnamon and Xylosweet mix). Add dry blend to wet and mix well.

Take mixture and roll little balls, then dip the top of the balls in the cinnamon/Xylosweet mix.

Place balls on baking sheet and bake for 16-18 min.

These cakes are delightful bite-size treats! They are mildly sweet, subtly spiced and perfect as a snack, a breakfast side or as a delicious complement to your afternoon tea.

WEEK Three

Shelved but Held

Day 15

"I waited patiently for the LORD; He turned to me and heard my cry."

(Psalm 40:1)

"Do you want me to hold you?" Darcē's (pronounced "Darsee") bushy tail wagged ferociously, shaking the entire back half of her tiny, white 5-pound body. As I leaned over to grab her, she grunted and sneezed, patted the ground with her front paws, then rolled over on her back in surrender, so excited about the idea of being held by her mommy. Effortlessly, I lifted her off the ground, placed her securely on her usual "perch" (i.e. resting on my right forearm with all her four legs dangling down the sides), then, I returned to my original duty of washing the dishes with my free hand. Throughout the chore, Darcē remained completely relaxed, eyes drooping, uninterestingly observing what her momma was doing, though she really didn't care. It didn't phase her when I leaned down to put dishes in the dishwasher; she paid no mind to my scrubbing the sink with bleach. And it didn't bother her that *she* was doing nothing "productive" at the moment, such as chasing a squirrel, barking at imaginary noises, or any of the other "tasks" of a typical "dog's day." She was just content to be on my arm; that was enough.

Eventually, I moved my arm, with Darcē still "on board," to the side, so I could continue my work and complete my tasks. Meanwhile, Darcē did nothing, at least, not until I put her down later, that is. She found perfect contented delight in being with me, and though her "life" was "shelved" for a while, the joy of being with me surpassed the thought or concern of getting back to her "duties."

This place of rest in the "shelved" state is what the Psalmist is referring to in the passage. The Word "patiently" is *Qâvâh*, which in the Hebrew means, "to bind (by twisting); to collect; to gather," as well as, "to endure, to hope, to trust; be confident in."[1] Waiting patiently on God is akin to being bound to Him, like a braid, constantly with Him while He performs His works, fulfills His plans, and does His will. However, our role may not come into play initially. Just as Darcē was "put to the side" while I worked, God sometimes does the same with us. He puts us "to the side" and continues working His plans, which may or may not include us for a while. We're not abandoned by Him, but we're seemingly not "moving forward" with our lives either.

You know this place. Have there ever been times when it seemed like everyone else was getting their breakthroughs, but you remained in your trial, and it even got a little worse? Those you prayed and warred for began rejoicing in their new deliverances and victories, but you were still stuck in your mess?

Shelved but Held

Day 15 (continued)

Have you ever cried out in frustration to God, "What about *me*?! When's it going to be *my* turn?!" We've all reached that place from time to time. On the one hand, we're happy for our friends and excited that our prayers are being answered ... yet on the other, we're frustrated, maybe even a little resentful toward God, though we dare not articulate it, because ... it just doesn't seem fair! After all, *we* prayed just as fervently as they did and God answered *their* prayers, as WELL as our prayers *for* them; so why not our prayers for *ourselves*? "Did You forget my request, Lord? Did You 'run out' of blessings right before You came to me? What's the big deal?"

Though it seems as if we are forgotten, the truth is we are actually closer to our Shepherd *while* we're waiting for His answer than we ever could be in any other time in our walks with Him. Being "put aside" in life is being placed on His arm, just as I placed Darcē on mine. It's being "gathered" to Him while He continues to do His work. God neither sleeps nor slumbers;[2] He is always at work behind the scenes, positioning all things into His perfect purposes. *You* may not be "moving forward" with your life at the moment; but that delay doesn't mean you won't fulfill your purposes, or that God has forgotten about them. On the contrary, God cannot forget you![3] Just as ridiculous as it would be for me to forget that I was holding Darcē, so it is equally absurd that God could forget about us. We are engraved on His hands,[4] ever before Him, and never abandoned by Him.

So then, since we are not forgotten, can we rest with that "patiently" of Ps. 40 while we wait? Can we be like Darcē, *excited* at the opportunity to be "put aside" from life, not concerning ourselves that our goals are not being reached, or that our breakthroughs are slow in coming, and just be thrilled at the idea of being held by our Daddy? I confess, it's not always easy to be so. It is far more natural to get frustrated when our lives are not "going anywhere." However, God is faithful. His Promises are "yes" and "amen" in Christ;[5] His plans are never thwarted.[6] The work He began in us will be completed,[7] but in His perfect timing. We can be confident of that.

Dear friend, if your life seems "on hold," if you feel as though you've been "put aside," and everyone else is moving forward with their dreams and goals and leaving you in the dust, don't despair. You are not forgotten by God; in fact, you are nearer to Him than you realize, safe in His grasp even now. Go ahead, adopt a "Darcē – like patience." Know that your life will move forward in time, your goals will be reached, and your purposes fulfilled. But for now, let it be enough to rest on your Daddy's arm.

Traditional Yellow Cake

YF

1-1/4 sticks	Butter *(softened)*
2/3 c.	Xylosweet
4	Large Eggs *(at room temperature)*
1	Egg Yolk *(at room temperature)*
1 c.	Coconut Flour *(sifted)*
1 tsp.	Baking Powder
1/8 tsp.	Salt
2/3 c.	Unsweetened Almond Milk
2 tsp.	Vanilla

Preheat oven to 350° F. In a bowl, with an electric mixer, beat the butter and sugar together for about 5 min. on medium high speed, until light and fluffy, scraping bowl occasionally. Add the egg yolk to the butter and Xylitol mixture and beat together until well blended. Add the rest of the eggs, one at a time, beating mixture after each addition.

In a separate bowl, combine all the dry ingredients together. Add the vanilla to the milk. With mixer on low speed, add the flour and milk to the butter and egg mixture. When all the milk and flour mixture is added, beat the cake batter together for about 5 min., until the color is a bit lighter and batter is light and fluffy.

Spoon the batter into the muffin cups and smooth out the tops. Bake for about 20 min., or until toothpick comes out clean. Makes about a dozen cupcakes. When cupcakes are completely cool, frost with **Powder-Puff Frosting** (see recipe). Enjoy!

Nessey TIPS

Because there is no yeast to hold the cake together, I typically just make cupcakes. Though I have never made a whole cake with this recipe (and don't recommend it), if you want to try it, here are the directions for doing so.

Grease 1 round 8 or 9 in. cake pan with coconut oil or butter, and dust with coconut flour. Follow all the other instructions as normal, but bake 30-35 min. or until toothpick comes out clean. To remove from pan: place the cake pan on a wire rack and let it cool for about 5 min. in the pan. Run a butter knife along the edges of the cake before removing it. Top with frosting once the cake has cooled.

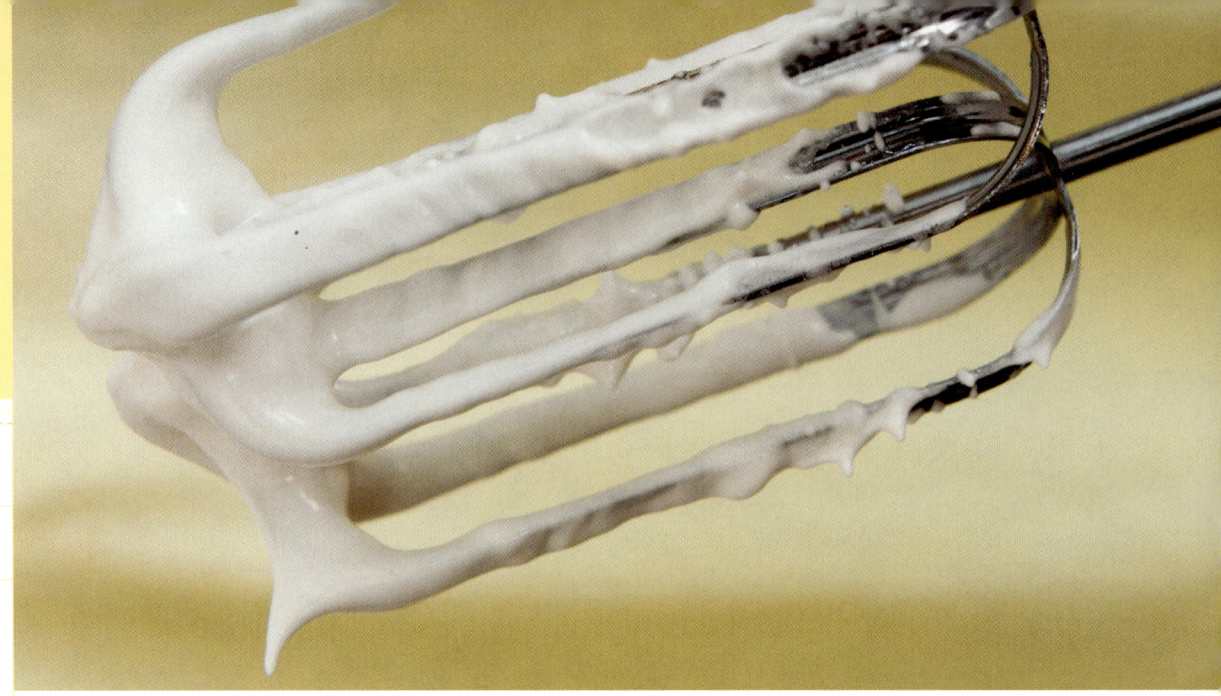

Nessey TIPS

For syrup: boil distilled water, and take 1-1/2 tsp. of it and place in a small bowl.

Add 6 tsp. of Xylosweet to water and stir together until a syrupy mix is created.

Double Boiler: *If you do not have a double boiler, all you have to do is use 2 pots, a small one that can fit into a larger one. Fill the larger pot with water and bring to a high boil for later use.

Powder-Puff Frosting

YK

3/4 c.	Xylosweet
1	Egg White
1-1/2 tsp.	Syrup *(see Nessey Tip)*
1/2 tsp.	Vanilla
1/4 tsp.	Salt
1/4 c.	Water

In top pot of double boiler,* using a mixer at high speed, beat all ingredients with ¼ c. water until blended (takes about 30 sec. to a min.). Once mixed, take pot and place over rapidly boiling water; beat at high speed until soft peaks form (takes about 4 min.). Pour into large bowl and beat until frosting is thick enough to spread. Fills and frosts 8 in. 2 layer cake and about a dozen cupcakes.

Flavor Varieties

Chocolate: Mix 6 Tbsp. unsweetened cocoa powder with 2 Tbsp. melted coconut oil and allow to cool. After making the original frosting, fold in melted chocolate.

Coconut: Prepare as normal, using ½ tsp. vanilla and ½ tsp. coconut extract. Spread final frosting on cake and sprinkle with unsweetened flaked/shredded coconut.

Peppermint: Prepare as normal, replace vanilla with 1/8 tsp. peppermint extract; tint pink with red food color.

"Though it seems as if we are forgotten, the truth is we are actually closer to our Shepherd while we are waiting for His answer."

Sufficient Grace

Day 16

We often hear and triumphantly quote the passage, *"My grace is sufficient for you, My power is made perfect in weakness."*[1] It brings us such comfort and inspiration! Moreover, we love to immediately follow this verse with another familiar passage, *"I can do all things through Christ, who gives me strength."*[2] Oh the victory and boldness we feel when we state these Scriptures together! We are boasting that God's grace (i.e. His empowerment for us to do what we could not do on our own)[3] is given to us to do, accomplish, achieve, and endure anything that may ever come our way! We've got what it takes, and we can do it all! At least, this is our most common interpretation of these passages.

But the Lord showed me something recently, which takes these verses to a different level of understanding. True, when we have responsibilities to meet, trials to endure, obstacles to overcome, and no human resources (from ourselves or from others) to do so, we *must* cling to God, who will strengthen us to walk out what *He's* placed before us. But that's the key: He gives us grace to accomplish what He's placed in front of us to accomplish. Thus, the question is, then, what is it that *He* has placed before us?

Have you ever come to a point in your life, in which you are "burning out," exhausted in more ways than one, "burning the candle at both ends," literally feeling like a hairline piece of thread ready to break, yet all the while claiming, "His grace is sufficient"? Many, if not all, of us have been in this place at one point in our lives, if not quite often. And I wouldn't doubt that some of you may be feeling this way right now. Between grocery store runs, cooking, cleaning the house, work responsibilities, deadlines, social events (some you might even host or organize), traveling, soccer practice, ballet recitals, school pageants, family reunions (and all the stress that those entail) ... (deep breath) ... then more cleaning, shopping - hitting the sales, church, classes, school functions, business meetings, conferences, doctor and dentist appointments, traffic, pets ... the word "exhaustion" merely scrapes the tip of the iceberg on how you are really feeling.

So, is this truly operating in God's grace? Sure, you were "superman/woman" being able to accomplish (or endure) the festivities and fiasco of your daily life, but how much of that was operating *within* the grace of God? Your feelings of exhaustion suggest bare minimum.

When we hear the aforementioned Scriptures, we immediately assume they infer that we are automatically enabled to do anything and everything that comes our way, almost as though we place God as a side margin note in our daily planners and schedules, labeling Him as "grace-fuel" for us to complete everything on our calendars. But burnout, exhaustion, stress – these are not the results, which someone would experience operating in the gift of God's grace. Rather, those are the results of operating in works.

"Ok, Jenness, so how do I know the difference? How can I know when I'm operating in grace and when I'm in works?" Good question, and one that I am still learning the answer to myself.

The Lord began to teach me a deeper principle about grace over one Thanksgiving Holiday. At the time, I was not doing well physically, and any additional stress, whether good or bad, had the potential to incur detrimental effects on my health. Thanksgiving was no exception. For that day, we (my parents and I) hosted the holiday meal in our home, and invited just three additional loved ones (family and a friend) to join us for the occasion. Unfortunately, what should have been a delightful event, seeing family, getting the house ready, taking part in games and conversation, proved too much for my body to handle. By midmorning, I started to go into

an adrenal crisis[3] and was forced to "lock" myself away in my room, away from the noise and energy of Thanksgiving cheer.

While laying in a fetal position on the floor, sobbing uncontrollably (not out of emotional distress, but as an outlet for the physical pressure and pain I was experiencing), unable to move (all muscle strength had left me), I cried out to God, "Lord! I don't have it (grace)! I can't leave my room ... I can't even get off the floor ..." I was bewildered, frustrated. His grace was "supposed" to be sufficient, so why couldn't I move? Why was it that I went into an Addisonian crisis, when He was "supposed" to have given me the strength to do what I couldn't do on my own, such as enjoy company, eat with my family, and celebrate the occasion? Where was His grace?!

As I lay there, the Spirit quietly spoke back the very Scripture I had just launched up to Him in my vexation, "My grace is sufficient for you ..." Now, when the Lord repeats anything, it is something important that needs your careful attention ... and when He repeats back to you exactly what you told Him, then you REALLY need to listen to what He's saying! Essentially, He was indicating that I had missed the point of this passage. Then, it clicked! "Jenness, I *have* given you sufficient grace to do all that *I've* called you to do on this day. If the grace is not there, then I haven't called you to it. *You* want My grace to include you being apart of the festivities downstairs; but *I* have called you to the quietness of your room today. You have sufficient grace to be in Me and rest in your room, where you will experience peace and joy in My presence. This is My grace for you on this day. Do not leave the boundaries of My sufficient grace." The strength I had for that day was enough to accomplish His "plans" for my Thanksgiving, rather than mine. By remaining in His presence and in quietness for the day, my adrenal crisis subsided, my body calmed down, and I was able to "recoup" from the episode without additional medical attention. However, my adrenal crisis might not have even occurred had I sought Him first on what *He* had purposed for me to do that day: a missed opportunity I do not intend to miss again.

> I have given you sufficient grace to do all that I've called you to do today. If the grace is not there, then I haven't called you to it.

When the Lord promises sufficient grace, He's not giving us a "blank check" of energy and resources to accomplish all of *our* plans and goals. Rather, He's giving us a specific amount of strength/resources for the tasks that *He* has called us to accomplish. You know you are operating within your "budget" of grace when you are walking in peace, in rest, and in joy. What should have been difficult is remarkably easy; and you find yourself operating efficiently and effectively in ways that can only be explained as enabled by God. When you begin to experience the symptoms of burnout, frustration, exhaustion and stress, *this* is when you have overextended His grace and have stepped into works.

Be assured, God's grace is sufficient; He will enable and equip you to do what you cannot do, just remember: His grace is budgeted for *His* plans for you, not yours. "In Him" is where we find sufficient grace.

Coco-Cupcakes

Coco-Cupcakes | YF

1/2 c.	Butter *(softened)*
1/3 + 1/2 c.	Xylosweet
5	Eggs *(at room temperature)*
1/4 tsp.	Vanilla
1 c.	Coconut Flour *(sifted)*
1/2 c.	Unsweetened Cocoa Powder
3/4 tsp.	Baking Soda
1/4 tsp.	Baking Powder
1/2 tsp.	Salt
2/3 c.	Unsweetened Almond Milk

Preheat oven to 350° F.

In an electric mixer, combine butter and Xylosweet (if you have a paddle attachment, use it): beat together for about 2 min. Add eggs in one at a time and beat high speed for about 3 min. Add vanilla while beating the eggs and butter mixture.

In a separate bowl, combine the dry ingredients together. Then, add flour to butter mix, alternating with milk. Beat batter for about 5 min. on high speed. Spoon batter into muffin cups (makes about 12-15). Bake for about 26-30 minutes. Allow cupcakes to cool completely before frosting. Frost with Chocolate version of the **Powder-Puff Frosting** (see recipe).

Nessey TIPS

Round Cakes:
(See *Nessey Tips* for **Traditional Yellow Cake** on page 60). For a regular cake, grease an 8 or 9 in. round cake pan with butter or coconut oil and dust with cocoa powder. Prepare batter as normal, spoon batter into prepared cake pan (smooth out top), and bake for 30-35 min. or until toothpick comes out clean. Frost after cake has cooled completely.

The Joy of Tribulation

Day 17

Many of us know this familiar passage:

"Consider it pure joy, my brothers, whenever you face trials of many kinds, because you know that the testing of your faith develops perseverance. Perseverance must finish its work so that you may be mature and complete, not lacking anything" (Jms. 1:2-4).

Now, the initial interpretation of this passage is exactly what it's talking about: we can consider it pure joy when we face hardships because the Lord is fashioning His character in us, He is completing His work in us, and He is preparing and equipping us for the calls that He has placed on our lives, so that we will be "full and complete, lacking nothing." Lacking nothing! Think about that! No lack, no need, no desire unfulfilled. In essence, the tribulation will expedite the process of us coming to a place of COMPLETE and TOTAL fulfillment in Christ, in our hearts, and in our lives! What an INCREDIBLE promise.

But there's another joy, which is not specifically stated in this passage that I believe anyone, who has ever faced the deepest valleys and sought the face of God in them, has come to understand, experience, and appreciate ... it is the joy of God's *Presence* in the suffering! To me, this is *really* what James was talking about. We can count it all joy when we face trials of all kinds, not only because of the character that He is fashioning *in* us, but more so because of the joy it is to be *with* Him **in His presence** in the process! He is *near* the broken-hearted; and the afflicted He does not despise, but listens and answers their cries![1] For where the Spirit of the Lord is, there is liberty, there is life, there is love, joy, peace, and all His other fruits as described in Galatians 5.

It is not that we *have* to go through hard times to appreciate His presence. In fact, He makes Himself available to us at all times, giving us complete access to His throne because of Christ.[2] However, there is something extra special, an extra tenderness and kindness that manifests from Him for those, who are suffering: an intimate embrace awaits the broken-hearted, the wounded and the afflicted, the weary and distressed. He is our Healer, our Keeper and our Comforter. But we cannot receive comfort if there is nothing needing to be comforted. We cannot be "kept" if there is nothing to keep. There is no need for healing if there is nothing to heal, right?

Oh for the joy of being with Him in the process of the pain! Like a mother, who holds, rocks, and soothes her child, who scraped his knee; like a mother hen, who gathers her chicks beneath her feathers, this place of vulnerability and strength under God's wings and in His arms is such a precious gift for us to cherish! My prayer is that you can find this same place with Him during the worst of times, because it is in these darkest and coldest of moments that the light of the Morning Star shines all the more brightly, and His warmth invades and surrounds our hearts more prominently.

To Him be the glory and honor and power forever!

> But there's another joy, which is not specifically stated in this passage ... it is the joy of God's *Presence* in the suffering!

5 Flavored Pound Cake

YF

1 c.	Butter
1 c.	Xylosweet
5	Eggs
1 c.	Unsweetened Almond Milk *(split into 1/2 c.)*
1 c.	Coconut Flour *(sifted)*
1 tsp.	Baking Powder
1 tsp.	Vanilla Extract
1 tsp.	Butter Extract
1 tsp.	Almond Extract
1 tsp.	Coconut Extract
1 tsp.	Maple Extract *(or lemon)**

Preheat oven to 375° F.

Cream butter and Xylosweet. Add eggs one at a time, beating after each. Mix flour and baking powder. Add dry to wet mix gradually, alternating with milk. Add ⅓ of the dry to wet mix while beating, then add ½ c. of the milk, continuing to beat the mix. Then, add another ⅓ of the dry, still beating, following with the last ½ c. of milk. Pour in the last of the dry and beat all ingredients together, mixing well.

Add in the extracts one at a time, stirring after each one; mix well. Grease and flour a 9 inch loaf or tube pan, and pour in mix. Bake for 1 hr., or until toothpick comes out clean, and/or edges have pulled away from pan. Store the cake in the fridge (in Tupperware).

Nessey TIPS

You can add syrup, which will give a sweeter taste, and make the cake richer and more moist. To do this, dissolve 1 c. of Xylosweet in 1/4 c. boiling water. Add 1/2 tsp. of each extract you used in the cake. Poke holes in the bottom of the cake. Then, with a spoon, drizzle the syrup into the holes. You do **NOT** use all of the syrup; probably between 1/2 to 1 Tbsp. of syrup, depending on how syrupy you want your cake to be. Also, you can drizzle a little syrup on top of the cake as well, once removed from the pan.

*Most pound cakes use lemon extract; sometimes I use maple extract instead.
For a more subtle pound cake, simply use vanilla and one other extract, such as butter or lemon.

In the Will

Day 18

There is a particularly popular doctrine, which is good and encouraging, but which I have found to be incomplete in its teaching. This is going to be a hard topic to swallow, especially for those of us, who have been raised in the American Culture of ease and consumerism, because all of us, to one extent or another, do not want to suffer in anyway.

Now, this is not necessarily a bad thing: we don't want to suffer because it is uncomfortable, painful, and can be extremely life-altering. Moreover *some* suffering does *not* even *hint* at being productive in our lives. It can be *extremely* difficult to see the "good" in trials when you suffer a miscarriage, your child is killed in a tragic accident, when you are diagnosed with advanced cancer, when your teen son or daughter comes home and tells you he or she is a drug-addict or pregnant, or when you learn that your spouse has been having an affair and wants a divorce. Nothing about these situations is good at their onset! Hardships like these are direct consequences of the Fall of man. However, let us consider something. If God knows all, is all powerful, and is always present, wouldn't He have previously known that the Fall would happen? Was He powerless to prevent it? Was it against His will that sin entered the world?

I have noticed that, a lot of times, we are so quick to suggest that suffering is not in God's will for our lives. Is this accurate when we take a closer look at who He is? To say that difficulties and trials are not in His will is to limit His sovereignty. It is to say that God has no control over our tragedies, that He was "caught by surprise" when our difficulty emerged. But God, the Almighty Everlasting Father of the Universe, *cannot* be without the power or knowledge to know or do anything about suffering.

My challenge to you today is to take a step out of any previous beliefs regarding suffering, and step up to a wider perspective, from God's vantage point.

Observe the following passage:

"Yet it was the LORD's will to crush Him and cause Him to suffer, and though the LORD makes His life a guilt offering, He will see His offspring and prolong His days, and the will of the LORD will prosper in His hand" (Isa. 53:10).

Now this is an interesting statement. Naturally, this is talking about Jesus and His crucifixion, but let's just ponder what the verse is suggesting. It be-

> A lot of times, we are so quick to suggest that suffering is not in God's will for our lives. Is this accurate when we take a closer look at who He is?

gins by saying, basically, that it was God's will for this Servant, His Son, to suffer. That doesn't sound very consistent with a God of love, does it? How could God "desire" His Servant to suffer? Look at the verses in another translation:

*"But the LORD was **pleased** to crush Him, putting Him to grief..."* (Isa. 53: 10 NASB)

It **pleased** God to allow His Child to suffer? Wow; but why? We have to be very careful when we read this verse because we may take it to the extreme that God delights in causing His children harm. Let's combat that with another verse:

"Yet the LORD longs to be gracious to you; He rises to show you compassion" (Isa. 30:18).

This verse clearly states that God is full of compassion and mercy, longing to bestow His love and tenderness on His children. So, granted, the Lord

is *not* "out to get" people and cause them to suffer. However, as the first passage suggests, sometimes, it *is* God's will for suffering to take place in our lives. Look at the next part of Isa. 53:10:

"... though the LORD makes His life a guilt offering, He will see His offspring and prolong His days, and the will of the LORD will prosper in His hand" (53:10b,c).

Now this suggests that the suffering has a purpose, doesn't it? "Though the Son was caused to suffer, the Son would see a better end" (paraphrase). The Lord desired the Son to suffer *because* He saw something on the other *side* of the suffering, which could only be reached *if* Jesus went *through* the pain of His sacrifice. What was on the other side? Prosperity, effectiveness in God's Kingdom, honor, fame, fullness of life, and, best of all, the restored relationship with His lost Beloved, meaning **us**!!! Christ would see the essence of Paul's statement to the Corinthians:

"... we do not lose heart. Though outwardly we are wasting away, yet inwardly we are being renewed day by day. For our light and momentary troubles are achieving for us an eternal glory that far outweighs them all" (2 Cor. 4:16-17).

Paul is inferring here that there is something far beyond our wildest dreams *after* our suffering is complete. Jesus saw it, *"Jesus, the Author and Perfecter of our faith, who for the joy set before Him endured the Cross, scorning its shame, and sat down at the right hand of the throne of God ..."* (Heb. 12:2)

Does this mean that Jesus *liked* the suffering? NO! The Bible says that He wept bitterly, sweating great drops of blood when His Father in Heaven led Him to be crucified.[1] He pleaded with the Father to find another way ... but there was no other way. There was no other way for God to establish His Son to obtain His full potential unless He went *through* the shame, suffering, and death. The Lord knew the ultimate purpose for His Son, to reign above all heaven and earth, and He *longed* for Jesus to "get there;" but that meant Jesus had to endure hardship first.

This illustration is an obvious one. In fact, in referring to Jesus's pain and hardship, many fellow brothers and sisters in Christ have suggested that Christ did all the suffering for us so that we won't have to endure it at all. To some extent, they are right.

*"He was wounded for **our** transgressions, He was bruised for **our** iniquities: the chastisement of **our** peace was upon Him; and with His stripes **we** are healed"* (Isa. 53:5).

Yes, this does express that there are some aspects of hardships in this life that Christ came to deliver us from them. I believe that God desires to heal us of our brokenness, emotionally, physically, and especially spiritually. That is the essence of what this verse is saying. But to say that this verse means that *all* our suffering will be eliminated because it's not God's will is taking it a little too far. Jesus promised that we would have trouble and persecution in this world (Jn. 16:33). It is the nature of this life at the present. Moreover, Jesus did not exclude His servants from suffering while they were right smack dab in the middle of God's will either.

· Stephen was stoned (Acts 7:54-60).
· James was beheaded (Acts 12:2).
· Peter was crucified upside down (Jn. 21:19).
· John was exiled on the Isle of Patmos (Rev. 1:9).
· All the other disciples were imprisoned, tortured, and/or martyred (Heb. 11:37-39).
· Paul suffered all kinds of torment and persecution for his faith (2 Cor. 6:3-13).
· Paul even had a thorn, which the Lord refused to remove (2 Cor. 12:6-10).

Could the Lord have prevented these things

In the Will

Day 18 (continued)

from happening or could He have intervened in the process? ABSOLUTELY! But He chose not to for reasons that only He can comprehend.

Notice how I inserted Paul's thorn in his side. I don't want you to think that it is only God's will that we suffer persecution and that no other suffering is permitted. This isn't an accurate depiction of the whole of Scripture. Consider Job. Why did the Lord present him, this righteous man, to the devil and allow the enemy to ransack everything that Job held dear? Let me propose something: how many of you have been encouraged by Job's story? Would Job have even been known to you had his life not been subject to so much pain and agony? Probably not. His story of wealth and righteousness might never have *even* been written down. But what is so encouraging? The fact that he suffered? NO! It's in the joy on the other side, in God's redemption of all that he lost. This is where we find so much encouragement to continue running this race of life!

And Job's hardships are not the only stories that encourage us. Joseph, Ruth, David, and countless others, all of their stories and their lives consist of heartache, pain, dismay, and torment. But what happens in the end of each of them? The Lord brings them into a place of glory that they could never have imagined! Joseph would never have ruled Egypt if he had not been betrayed. Ruth could never have been redeemed by Boaz if she had not been widowed. David would never have been king unless he was placed into a hostile working environment. These men and women went through years of confusion, loss, pain, depression, and anxiety. Years of emotional torment and fear. They all suffered greatly, but they were still in God's will! Why? Because He saw where He was taking them ... and He promised to take them *through* to get to that place.

Ok, some of you might be thinking, "Well, that's great, but what would someone like you know about suffering? You don't know what I'm going through and you can't relate to my situation." I'm not going to argue with that—in fact, it is true that I cannot in any way possibly know exactly what you're going through and feel what you are feeling. But I *can* tell you. I do know what it means to suffer.

I have suffered rejection and persecution for my faith. I have been betrayed and wrongfully accused, judged, and deserted. I have endured an illness that has ripped a decade of my youth away. I have suffered relentless physical pain, incessant nausea, and unending frailty to the point that I could not even walk on my own. I have been all over the States, visiting countless doctors who'd accuse me, spiritual leaders, who'd condemn me, and even myself at times wondering at my own sanity. My life has been completely turned upside down from what it used to be as a result of suffering.

Despite it all, never once have I questioned God's love for me. Why? Because I *know* Him and that He is doing something. When tragedy strikes, I refer to His promise. When depression hits, I cling to His faithfulness. When everything seems to fail, I reach for His strength. I *know* God is faithful! I *know* that He will redeem my life and that my latter days will be greater than those light and momentary days of affliction. How do I know? Because what He did for Jesus, He can do for me! What He did for Job, Joseph, Ruth, and David, He can do for me also. And what He can and will do for me, He can and will do for you too!

Don't reject the suffering as if it isn't God's will. Don't question His power and His sovereignty in the process of your refinement. God loves you. He wants to do great things in and through you. And He will, by bringing you to that place — on the other side of your suffering.

Nessey's Ice Cream

YF

- **1 c.** Xylosweet
- **2 c.** Nessey's Heavy Cream *(see recipe page 77)*
- **1 c.** Unsweetened Almond Milk
- **2** Eggs
- **1-1/2 tsp.** Vanilla Extract
- **1 Tbsp.** Lemon Juice

1) In a medium skillet on low heat, stir Xylosweet, milk, and eggs. Cook, stirring continuously until mixture thickens and coats back of a metal spoon (10-20 min.). Remove from heat and let cool.

2) In a medium bowl, whip cream with electric mixers until soft peaks form. "Fold" cream into cooled mix and allow to refrigerate for 8 hrs (or overnight).

3) Stir chilled mix then freeze in an ice cream maker. If you do not have an ice cream maker, pour mix into a "freezer safe" container, put in freezer, wait 45 min., then take it out and stir it vigorously (to break up icing crystals) using an electric stir stick or wire whisk.

4) Return it to freezer, wait 30 min., then take it out and stir again. Repeat this process every 30 min. for the next 2-3 hrs. until the ice cream is completely solidified.

Nessey TIPS

Flavor options:
For chocolate flavor, add 2 Tbsp. (or to taste) of unsweetened cocoa powder to mix and use 3/4 tsp. of vanilla.

For an even more "chocolaty" taste, use Chocolate Almond milk.

Blessed Obedience

Day 19

When the Lord tells you to do something, you have a choice to make: A) Do it right away; or B) Don't. We know for a fact that disobedience leads to a curse,[1] so naturally, we'd *want* to obey everything the Lord tells us because the opposite of that curse is being blessed ... who *doesn't* want to be blessed? Therefore, if you do what He asks you to do, you walk in obedience, and the blessings/rewards are countless, right? That's what we'd rightly conclude.

But what does that actually mean? "**Blessed**," as the Amplified version of the Bible describes it, is "Happy, fortunate, and to be envied."[1] Who *doesn't* want THAT?! Who doesn't want others to envy

> Sometimes God doesn't come through like you thought He should have.

what we have because our lives are so happy and fortunate? But I think, at least, I've noticed in my life and my own personal tendencies, we take this to an extreme. We make assumptions on what we think "blessed" is supposed to look like in our lives. For example, God tells you to do something, and you know that there's reward in obedience, so you do it ... do you expect a certain outcome? Do you expect that, say, if you pray for your co-workers or peers that are awful to you, that you will receive something from God in return? I'm not saying you won't receive something from God; but what I'm asking is: are you expecting to receive something *specific*? Such as, "Ok - I'll pray for this person, and the Lord will give me that promotion I've been asking Him for."

Let me take this a step further: say you've been *pleading* with God for something for a looooonnnggg time: you need a financial breakthrough. One day in your prayer time, you sense the Lord calling you to a fast. So you fast ... is it not natural that you'd expect God to give you that financial breakthrough? Sometimes He will, but if you walk with the Lord long enough, you discover that sometimes ... He *doesn't* come through in answer to your obedience like you thought He would have, or "should" have, for that matter.

Several years ago, I was believing God for a miracle, a miraculous healing for my body. One night, after tears and deep weeping, I felt the Lord call me to do something that was almost impossible for me to do physically: travel to another state and attend a ministerial conference. The plans were made, the reservations set, and by the grace of God, my family and I made it to this conference. I attended every session, just "knowing" I was going to be healed. There were even special times of prayer when the main speaker prayed for healing for those who were ill that were present, and OH! Was I the MOST faith-filled and expectant during those prayers! After all, that's why I was there! God told me to go to the conference during my petition for the miracle; so naturally I assumed that meant He was going to heal me there. The conference ended, we packed our things, flew home, with me still in pain, still in a wheelchair ... and still as weak and ill as ever. In fact, I had to spend a couple of weeks afterwards just *recovering* from going to this event ... did God not fulfill His promise? Did God not "bless" me for my obedience?

Like me, I'm sure you've hit these crises of belief: you come to a crossroads in your faith where you've done *everything* God told you to do, and yet it seems He either ignores you or abjectly refuses to answer/fulfill His promise of blessing you for your obedience. What gives? Why don't our situations turn out the way we thought they should?

What the Lord showed me was that it's a matter of interpretation. "'*For My thoughts are not your thoughts. Neither are your ways My ways,*' declares the Lord. '*For as the heavens are higher than the earth, so are My ways higher than your ways, and My thoughts than your thoughts*'" (Isa. 55:8-9).

Our idea of what "blessed" means is, more often than not, COMPLETELY different from God's interpretation of the term. We think that we are blessed if God answers our "obedience" in the way *we* think He should: like me receiving a miraculous healing at that conference, or you receiving a promotion at work for being kind to the nastiness that sits in the cubicle across from you, or that financial miracle for fasting, as God had directed. But being "blessed" is infinitely more glorious than just receiving the answers to our initial prayers. It goes so much deeper; it's richer, fuller, more than an answer to our current situation.

God doesn't look at you and your situation now. He looks at you now, *and* next week, *and* next year, decade ... as well as the lives of ALL the people, with whom you will come in contact in the years to come. He takes it ALL into perspective, measures it, weighs it, and decides how best to "bless" you and those around you for your obedience.

Did you know, had I received that miracle when I wanted it, I would NEVER have considered writing a book? I would never have walked into the open doors that are beginning to open up now, would never have met the people I have met over the course of my illness? The contacts, the life experiences, all of it would have been thwarted. The things in my life that have DEEPLY blessed me since that time at the conference would never have occurred had I been healed then. And that's just scratching the surface! I can't tell you how humbling it is to know how many people have been blessed by these devotionals I have written in response to my illness. It boggles my mind to hear the stories of people, who are drawn into the presence of God in prayer because they feel a burden to pray for me. The countless believers and nonbelievers who have been inspired and encouraged by the battle I have waged with this ailment.

God **has** blessed me for my obedience to Him in ways I couldn't have possibly imagined during those cool autumn days at that conference ... what about you? How has God blessed you for NOT answering your obedience in the way you thought He would? How has your relationship with Him deepened? What new friendships have developed? What lives have been touched? What future opportunities are in store because you DO obey your Father in Heaven?

Blessed, happy, fortunate, and to be envied are we who obey the Lord ... how true this promise is.

> Being "blessed" is infinitely more glorious than just receiving the answers to our prayers.

Nessey's Coco-Fudge Pie

Nessey's Coco-Fudge Pie | YF

Nessey TIPS

1	9" Baked Piecrust *(see recipe)*
1 c.	Xylosweet
1/2 c.	Unsweetened Cocoa Powder
2 c.	Unsweetened Almond Milk
7 Tbsp.	Coconut Flour
1 pinch	Salt
2	Egg Yolks
1/2 Tbsp.	Butter Extract
1 tsp.	Vanilla
1 Tbsp.	Butter

Mix Xylosweet, cocoa, milk, flour, salt, egg yolks, and butter flavoring in medium saucepan and cook until thick. Add vanilla and butter, remove from heat.

Allow to cool.

Put in baked pie crust and cool in refrigerator. Can be served alone, or you can top individual pieces with **"Whip Cream"** (see **Nessey's Heavy Cream** recipe) prior to serving.

For the chocoholic, you can make this a "Double Fudge" pie by using chocolate almond milk in the recipe, if you dare.

Nessey TIPS

Something to note on the **Whip Cream**: This whip cream does not "stand" very long; it will melt much like ice cream after a while. If you are making it as a topping for a pie, or as a dip for fruit, make it for <u>individual pieces</u> of pie (**not** <u>the whole pie</u>), and whenever you serve it, eat it <u>immediately</u>. It's very tasty, but it's not meant to be (nor can be) "preserved."

Nessey's Heavy Cream

YF

3/4 c. Unsweetened Almond Milk

1/2 c. Unsalted Butter

Heat together in a skillet on low heat until butter melts into milk. Do not boil.

Pour into blender (must be blender in order to get air into mixture), and blend on highest speed for 3 min.

Refrigerate for at least 24 hrs. and use for recipes or whip cream.

To use as **Sweetened Whip Cream**, after it has chilled, bring out mix and add 2 ½ Tbsp. Xylosweet and 1 tsp. vanilla for every cup of heavy cream; whip as you would whip cream.

For **Chocolate Whip Cream**, also add 2 Tbsp. unsweetened cocoa for every cup of heavy cream (and for Double Chocolate Whip Cream: use chocolate almond milk in original **Heavy Cream** recipe).

Almond Pastry Pie Crust

YF

Nessey TIPS

To avoid burning the crust, take a thin strip of aluminum foil and wrap just the top edge of the crust to cover it.

- 1/4 c. Butter *(softened)*
- 1/4 c. Xylosweet
- 1 Egg Yolk
- 2 c. Almond Flour *(finely ground)*

Combine Xylosweet with butter and egg yolk. Using a blender, gradually mix in flour until crumbs form.

Roll into a dough ball. Grease pie plate with butter. Press dough into bottom and up sides of a 9-inch pie plate.

For "baked piecrust" recipes, bake at 400° F for about 10 minutes, or until edge is browned. Cool and follow pie instructions.

For unbaked, leave as is and follow pie instructions.

The Worst of Times ...

Day 20

One of the things I have learned over the course of my illness was that many times, the best of times were actually in the worst of times, though circumstances and emotions claimed otherwise. I came to discover that the worst of times, both emotionally and circumstantially, were the seasons, in which the grace for doing what I had been doing began to lift, and I'd reach this unbearable point of breaking, screaming, "I CAN'T DO THIS ANYMORE!" It was the lowest point emotionally/spiritually/mentally/even physically ... but it was one of my best moments as well.

What do I mean by "the grace"? God gives us the grace to persevere and/or do whatever it is He has required us to do, whether that be performing one's daily activities, fulfilling one's responsibilities, or going through a trial of some kind with a strength and tenacity that we don't understand and could never claim as our own. Grace is His strength and mercy that empowers us to continue to accomplish tasks, bear fruit, and maintain a positive outlook and/or our faith in His goodness, which, to an observer (and even ourselves), appears ridiculous and impossible.

That's why, many times, you will find people doing these great feats, enduring incredible adversity, and yet, they are still functioning. They're not just surviving, but they are actually somehow *living* ... and with gladness! So you marvel, "Wow! How in the world can you do all that? How can you raise 6 boys and suffer from chronic fatigue and hormonal imbalances? How can you continue to smile and be joyful following a painful divorce and the sudden death of your son? How in the world can you run a growing nonprofit organization while simultaneously being an active leader in your church, serving and loving countless needy people from all over the REGION, and yet still be a caretaker for a critically ill child at home?" Quite frankly, they can't! At least, not on their own. They are only able to beat incredible odds because they are walking in the grace the Lord has given them.

But there comes a point when the grace begins to wane. You don't know when this point will hit until, all of the sudden, your ability to cope and do what you've been doing starts to dissipate. You find yourself becoming increasingly weary of the process. Now, this is not to say that you won't have ups and downs emotionally throughout the process *with* the grace. We are emotional beings, and we will grow weary in the battle from time to time. But the Lord is faithful to give us His sufficient grace that lifts us out of our "hole" and places us on our feet again to continue fighting the good fight and running the

> It was my lowest point emotionally, spiritually, mentally, even physically ... but it was one of my best moments as well.

race. I'm not talking about these vacillating moments of weariness throughout the ordeal. I'm talking about a progressive, wearying sense that starts as a quiet whisper in your spirit, and an ever so small flicker of a thought; but gradually, the whisper becomes louder, more and more noticeable. From whisper, to mutter, from mutter, to statement, from statement to directive, from directive to a shout. That feeling of, "... I ... can't ... do ... this ..." It is these

are the Best of Times

times that I am referring to: these are the best/worst of times.

The grace is waning. It suddenly occurs to you that what you've been doing, you just can't do much longer. You're tired. You're feeling this closing in claustrophobic sensation, a sinking, trapped imprisonment crouching in, where all you want to do

> The Lord is "weaning" you off of the grace He's been providing because you are about to make a transition to a new place in your circumstance, in which you won't need that grace anymore.

is curl up in a fetal position and hide from life, hide from the circumstance or problem, stop everything and bury yourself in the ground.

What makes matters worse ... you know you can't. You can't run away from an illness that is ransacking your body. You can't just pull the plug on your mother/fatherhood responsibilities. You can't stop working at that job that is providing for your family. You can't stop, but oh! You WANT to! You wish it would all disappear, vanish, be done, pinch me and wake me up from this nightmare. If only life could be solved with a wish to a magic genie and poof! The trial is gone!

This is the point when it seems there's no light at the end of the tunnel. But actually, the end of the tunnel is closer than you can imagine. The grace is lifting because the Lord is getting ready to reposition you from doing what you *have* been doing to doing something else. His all sufficient grace was to get you *through* the valley, but not to leave you *in* the valley. His grace was like the manna in the desert, miraculous provision to get you through the wilderness, but the manna ceases once you cross into the Promise Land.[1] The Lord is "weaning" you off of the grace He's been providing because you are about to make a transition to a new place in your circumstance, in which you won't *need* that grace anymore.

Now, I can't tell you when that transition will be or what it will look like. Sometimes, it means making changes in your schedule to operate in the level of grace the Lord is providing. Other times, it might be that you make some other changes, such as switching to a different doctor, or becoming more involved in church activities. It could also possibly mean that the Lord is about to do a miracle in your life and deliver you completely. We don't know *what* the change will be, but rest assured, a change is coming and will be sooner than you think.

Know this: while you are in the transitional period, the tears will continue to fall and increase in number, your tension will keep rising, you will feel as though your emotions will burst and shatter, and you will start to believe that you have never in your life been in so much agony as at this moment in time. But *don't lose heart*! This worst time in the season is your best time in the season because it means you are at the nearest point to the *end* of the season than you've ever been before! A breakthrough is right around that corner. And once His grace ceases, you will have emerged victorious.

Nessey's Peanut Butter Pie

Nessey's Peanut Butter Pie | YF

1	9" Baked Piecrust *(see recipe)*
1 c.	Xylosweet
1/2 c. + 2 Tbsp.	Unsweetened Peanut Butter *(crunchy or creamy)*
2 c.	Unsweetened Almond Milk
1/2 c. + 1 Tbsp.	Coconut Flour
1 pinch	Salt
2	Egg Yolks
1/2 Tbsp.	Butter Extract
1 tsp.	Vanilla
1 Tbsp.	Butter
1/2 c.	Chopped Peanuts *(optional)*

Mix Xylosweet, peanut butter, milk, flour, salt, egg yolks, and butter flavoring in medium saucepan and cook until thick. Add vanilla and butter. Remove from heat.

Allow to cool.

Put in baked pie crust and cool in refrigerator. Can be served alone, or you can top individual pieces with **Whip Cream** (see **Nessey's Heavy Cream** recipe), sprinkle with chopped peanuts, then serve!

Nessey TIPS

You will have extra filling left over, which makes an EXCELLENT **Fruit Dip**! Serve with apple slices and/or celery sticks. YUM!!!

Catalyst

Day 21

And you will be called priests of the LORD, you will be named ministers of our God.

(Isa. 61:6)

I'm sure you've often heard the phrase, "Life's not all about you," a time or two in your life. It's true – life is not all about us. But sometimes, when you're in the middle of something traumatic in your life, say you had to foreclose on your dream home, or you get laid off at work; perhaps you haven't heard from your son all day, and late that evening you hear the ominous ring of a late night call – he's been arrested; maybe you come home late from work, and instead of walking into the aroma of a prepared meal, you are welcomed by an eerie silence and a note on the counter: your wife has gone to her mother's with the kids and won't be back … don't you feel somewhat justified in desiring that, for one moment, life *could* be about you? Just for a moment!

"Why can't we talk about what *I* want from life, how *I* was wanting today to turn out to be like. After all, I've spent my life giving and pouring myself into the lives of others. I've faithfully followed the precepts of Christ, obeying Him at every turn, standing in faith through crisis after crisis … and for *what*?!" Yes, there comes a point in the journey of perseverance when we begin to think, "God! Can't it be about *me* this time? Can't we stop everything for a moment and fix my problem now? I don't want to do this anymore … I'm tired of persevering, and waiting, and 'faithing' … I want something done about *my* circumstances right NOW! I know You have Your plan, but why can't we at least consider MINE for a change?!"

We all hit this juncture, some of us more often than others, but the result is still the same: cry as we might, passionately rant and rave our justification for our frustrations about why life hasn't been fair, no matter what we do — life will *still* not be about us. Gee, that's encouraging …

So, if it's not about us, then what is life about anyway? Oh, we won't delve too deeply into that concept. That's an age-old question that man has attempted to answer for generations. But let us view the idea in reference to the text in Isaiah for a moment. What does this say about us as believers? The Lord calls us His priests and ministers.

"*And you will be called priests of the LORD, you will be named **ministers** of our God*" (Isa. 61:6). So what does that mean exactly?

The word "ministers" in this text is the Hebrew word: *shârath*.[1] It is used to describe an individual, whose prime responsibility is to serve or attend a higher ranking individual, whether a public servant, officer, member of the royal family, or any other type of leader, like a servant, armor-bearer, or assistant. A "*shârath*" of God, however, is an individual characterized by priesthood, one who works in the temple, conducting the special tasks, performing sacred rituals, etc., as would be found in any type of worship setting. And still, while his temple tasks were important and required as part of his "job description" in serving his Master, performing sacrifices and walking around worshipping God all day in the temple building was NOT his ultimate function as a minister. On the contrary, a *shârath*'s *most important* duty was to complete these tasks so that he could provide *others* access to the presence of God!

Remember what Paul said about our High Priest/Minister Jesus?

"But now in Christ Jesus you who once were far away have been brought near through the blood of Christ ... For through Him we both have access to the Father by one Spirit ... Consequently, you are ... members of God's household" (Eph. 2:13,18-19).

Christ fulfilled performing the necessary commissions of His Master, which included shedding His blood, so that the people, who believed in Him, would have access to the Father. In other words, Christ's suffering, His ministry to the Father on earth, everything He did while He lived in the body, was not about Him: it was about providing a means for *everyone* to have access to a *relationship* with God.

That is the prime function of God's minister: serving God and making a way for others to come near to Him. This is the life, to which Christ was called, and to which *we* are called ...

You might be thinking, "Well, that's comforting in a way, but it does little to stifle the sting that life just dealt me. I mean, how can you say that it *ministers* to God when I hurt so badly?"

I, too, have pondered that same logic many times in light of the heartaches of so many brothers and sisters in the faith as well as in retrospect with my own trials. After all, it doesn't really sound like God is who He says He is, a loving Father, if what ministers to Him are the pains His children endure, right? What parent in their right mind would want their kid to be sick for so long, go through a painful divorce, or lose their job? However, and I know how hackneyed this may sound, but, we have to take one thing into account: God's ways *are* infinitely higher than our ways. In recognizing this, I have continued to press Him on this issue, "Lord, You are the essence of love and faithfulness ... so how do You justify allowing such difficult agonies to come upon Your people in light of Who You are?" In my searching, the Lord keeps answering me with one word: catalyst.

A catalyst is: "something that initiates or causes an important event to happen."[2] In regard to my illness, for example, while there are a myriad of blessings being born as a result of it (some of which have been shared), a major part of the reason for my season of affliction is that it serves as His catalyst to bring about an exceedingly more important event: drawing others to His throne of grace. In other words (to borrow a popular phrase), my pain is for another's gain.

Now, put your own circumstance into the mix: what you are suffering/enduring/facing right now — what if it too was a catalyst in God's redemptive plan of grace? Could you consider it being used as an essential element in God's gargantuan divine plan of reuniting man to Himself? Your predicament is not about you, but its main purpose is being used as an essential element in God's redemptive plan of reconciling man to Himself! Think about that! Your suffering is HIS tool to perform the ultimate miracle of divine grace!

Let's look at the reverse side of the equation: How often do you ask people to pray for you when everything is going well? Would you ever go up to your pastor or accountability partner and say something like, "Hey, I just won the lottery, would you pray for me that I enjoy my wealth?" Of course not! How ridiculous would that be?! On the contrary, we ask people for their prayers when we're in dire straits, right? Even *nonbelievers* ask for prayer when they are going through tough times!

Now here's the cream: what is prayer?

What if your circumstance was a catalyst in God's redemptive plan of grace?

Catalyst

Day 21 (continued)

It is communication with God! And how does communication take place? When one has access to His ear, and that comes in BEING IN HIS PRESENCE!!! God *desperately* desires communication and relationship with the people on earth! Why else would Christ tell so many parables that discuss this very aspect of God's nature, of Him leaving the many, who are safe, to go and find the one, who is lost? He deeply loves all, who have been made in His image; so much so that He would have died for ONE, just **ONE** in order to ransom him and invite him into His family! We can't even begin to fathom the depth of this love that God has for each and every one of us!

And once we do come into fellowship with the Lord, this is when He calls us His priests and ministers.[3] We are immediately granted the privilege of the position of "*shârath*" being named a minister to Him in His house (which is actually within us – His Spirit abiding in us[4]), serving Him daily, walking in His presence, and having free access to fellowship with our Master. And part of our duties? To make way for others to share and experience this same type of relational access and intimacy with our Father.

Now, how the Lord incorporates this position as part of His unique plan for our individual lives will vary. In my case, He's used a chronic illness to inspire and propel many believers and nonbelievers to come boldly to His throne with their prayers of intercession for my healing. Though healing seemed to evade me, the purpose of the suffering was not negated! In fact, the longer I remained ill, the more people went into God's presence on a regular basis. Deep relationships with the Lord have deepened. Estranged relationships between believers and their Father have been realigned. Some nonbelievers have come to a knowledge of His love and have been grafted into His family. And even a few hardhearted individuals (those, who would otherwise have little desire or interest in "religious" things) have been touched. This was not because of me, but it was on account of God's use of His catalyst, a *shârath* that performed her Master's commission by taking care of the menial tasks (i.e. calling people to prayer) so that many could come boldly to the Lord with access to His ever anticipatory ear, an ear that longs to hear the voices of His kids!

If my Master wishes to use an ailment to bring one sinner to Himself, then as His *shârath*, I will gladly lay down my plans and my agendas for my life so that His hopes and dreams are fulfilled! He is my Master, and my desire is to minister to Him in spirit and in truth.

And for you, as a fellow *shârath*, my prayer is that somehow the Lord would unveil in your heart a similar revelation of what it means to be His catalyst in light of your own circumstances. Have you considered that your son's arrest might actually bring someone to Christ? Have you considered that your job loss might have just answered a desperate prayer for one of your struggling brothers or sisters in the Lord, whom you don't know, who would have been on the streets in a matter of days had your job opening never happened?

Life is not about us. We know that; and knowledge of that reality doesn't offer a lot of comfort either; at least, not at first. But to know that what we're going through has a *purpose*? To consider our ordeals as catalysts for God's divine plan of redemption? Now *that's* something our hope can grab hold of! No matter what you're going through, no matter what enemies you face, storms you encounter, tornadoes of pain and confusion you endure ... **<u>IT IS NOT IN VAIN</u>**. Your ministry as *shârath* to your Master is serving a higher purpose. You are participating in God's ultimate destiny, desire, and hope for all the world: that ALL might have access to His presence. Be encouraged, minister of the Lord! Your pain *is* gain.

Carrot Pie

Y2F

1	9" Unbaked Pie Shell *(see recipe)*	
3/4 c.	Xylosweet	
2 c.	Chopped Carrots	
2	Eggs	
1 tsp.	Ground Cinnamon	
1 tsp.	Vanilla Extract	
3/4 c.	Unsweetened Almond Milk	

Preheat oven to 400° F. Press the pie crust into the bottom and up the sides of a 9 inch pie plate.

Bake the pie shell for 3 to 5 minutes, just to firm it up, then remove from oven, and set aside. Steam carrots until tender; about 10 minutes. Drain water. Puree carrots until smooth in a food processor.

In a medium bowl, mix together the Carrot Puree, Xylosweet, and eggs. Mix in cinnamon and vanilla. Gradually stir in milk. Pour the mix into the partially baked pie shell.

Bake for 10 min. in the preheated oven, then reduce heat to 350° F. Bake for another 40 to 45 min. at lower temperature, or until firm. Allow to cool, then serve!

Nessey TIPS

Remember, you can wrap aluminum foil over the edges of the pie crust to avoid burning.

This cake goes well with **Whip Cream** (see **Nessey's Heavy Cream** recipe) and makes an excellent substitute for pumpkin or sweet potato pie.

In Light of Eternity

Epilogue

In light of eternity, these trials we face are mere vapors; in light of eternity, the darkness that so overwhelms us is but a speck of sawdust when presented before the Light of the World.

In light of eternity, the joy of being in Christ's presence banishes the sorrows of "feeling" His absence. In light of eternity, the most fearful situation is an afterthought, the most difficult temptation, a footnote; the most horrid terror, a feather tossed aside by the winds of His wings. We are eternal beings in Christ. We live for today to glorify Him, but we will live in the long tomorrow to resonate Him! Can we grasp this? Can we stand in boldness of faith that our light and momentary afflictions are producing in us an exceeding weight of glory that far surpasses them all? Though our minds are somewhat limited, our hearts are unchained by the confines of mortal man's reasoning. We live in continuum of life to life, faith to faith, glory to glory, a gift that Christ paid dearly for us to enjoy. It's ours! Cherish this thought – your present circumstances – that mountain so immense and foreboding that seems impossible to climb or avert; that sorrow that weighs so heavily in your heart, as if it were lead ticking within your bosom; that terror so overwhelming that your entire body trembles at its consideration –

> We live in continuum of life to life, faith to faith, glory to glory, a gift that Christ paid dearly for us to enjoy. It's ours!

it is momentary … all of it. THAT THING that you are facing is temporal, but YOU, beloved, are eternal. You will go on, and your assaulter will bow the knee, subject under the all-sovereign name of the Lord, our Lord, the Lord of all, Jesus Christ; and through His blood, His name, His eternity, His victory, is now … yours.

Appendix

Endnotes

3. *It Comes with Benefits*: [1]Ps. 103:2-14
[2]Eph. 1:20-21, 2:6
[3]Col. 1:12
[4]Jn. 14:16, 26
[5]Eph. 3:20

4. *Spread Your Wings and Fly!*: [1]2 Cor. 2:15
[2]1 Cor. 6:11
[3]2 Cor. 5:21
[4]Rom. 6:11

5. *Growing*: [1]ref. Lk. 2:42
[2]ref. Jms. 1:2

6. *No More Rules!*: [1]ref. Isa. 53:5 & Rom. 8:2
[2]Matt. 5:17
[3]Gal. 3:13
[4]Jn. 10:10 (AMP)
[5]Heb. 10:10

7. *The One Who Leads Me*: [1]Not her real name
[2] Nâhăg'. 5090. *A Concise Dictionary of the Words in the Hebrew Bible*, by James Strong, in Spiros Zodhiates, ed., *The Hebrew-Greek Key Word Study Bible: Unlocking the Riches of God's Word (NASB)* (Chattanooga, TN: AMG Publishers, 1993), 73. Found in the following Scriptures: Deut. 4:27; Psalms 48:14; 78:53; 80:1; Isa. 63:14; Lam. 3:2.

8. *Did I Miss You?*: [1]The diagnosis for the root cause of my illness was Lyme Disease induced Adrenal Insufficiency, which took about 7+ years for doctors to finally conclude. However, as are the consequences of such an ailment, if it is not treated properly and immediately when the signs of "adrenal crises" develop, a patient will succumb to what is called an "adrenal crash." This means that, in the "crash," I would suffer from a myriad of additional conditions along with adrenal failure, including:

    Blood Sugar Abnormalities (associated with the pancreas)
    Chronic Fatigue (associated with low function of the thyroid)
    PCOS (Polycystic Ovarian Syndrome)
    POTS (Postural Orthostatic Tachycardia Syndrome-associated with the heart)
    Gilbert's Syndrome (dysfunction of the liver)

It was during these "crashes" that I had to treat every affected organ/system in addition to treating the adrenal glands and later Lyme Disease. These crashes were dangerous and took months to years to "pull out of;" but by the grace of God, I am still here! And I am still making every effort to continually live as incense before my Creator!

12. *Suffering for Righteousness*: ¹Rom. 4:3
    ²ref. Jms. 2:19
    ³ref. Mk. 5:36
    ⁴ref. Job 2:9

13. *The Coffin*: ¹Lk. 22:42
    ²ref. Eph. 1:20; 2:6

14. *Immovable Mountains*: ¹ref. Jn. 12:19

15. *Shelved but Held*: ¹Qâvâh. 6960. *Lexicon Aids to the Old Testament, in The Hebrew-Greek Key Word Study Bible: Unlocking the Riches of God's Word (NASB)* (Chattanooga, TN: AMG Publishers, 1993), 1771.
    ²ref. Ps. 121:4
    ³ref. Isa. 49:15
    ⁴ref. Isa. 49:16
    ⁵ref. 2 Cor. 1:20
    ⁶ref. Job 42:2
    ⁷ref. Phil.1:6

16. *Sufficient Grace*: ¹ref. 2 Cor. 12:9
    ²Phil. 4:13
    ³see *The Worst of Times are the Best of Times* (Day 20)
    ⁴see *Did I Miss You?* Endnote 1

17. *The Joy of Tribulation*: ¹ref. Ps. 51:17; Ps. 22:24
    ²ref. Heb. 4:16

18. *In the Will*: ¹ref. Lk. 22:44

19. *Blessed Obedience*: ¹Blessed. in *The Amplified Bible (AMP)* (Grand Rapids, MI: Zondervan, 1987), 1078.
    ²ref. Deut. 11:27-28

20. *The Worst of Times are the Best of Times*: ¹ref. Josh. 5:12

21. *Catalyst*: ¹Shârath. 8334. *Lexicon Aids to the Old Testament, in The Hebrew-Greek Key Word Study Bible: Unlocking the Riches of God's Word (NASB)* (Chattanooga, TN: AMG Publishers, 1993), 1790.
    ²Catalyst. (n.d.). Investopedia.com. Retrieved February 19, 2009, from Dictionary.com website: http://dictionary.reference.com/browse/catalyst
    ³ref. Isa. 61:6
    ⁴ref. 1 Cor. 6:19, Jn. 14:17

Bibliography

The following books, cookbooks, and reference works were either used or referenced throughout the course of my illness for personal study and education. However, with the exception of the Scriptures and unless otherwise noted, the information compiled within *Nessipees* is original summations of the information I have obtained from numerous publications including the following as well as countless unlisted others found elsewhere, such as from the internet. I have tried to list at least some personally significant sources, which have contributed to my current knowledge.

Balch, James F., M.D. and Phyllis A. Balch, C.N.C. *Prescription for Nutritional Healing: A Practical A-Z Reference to Drug-Free Remedies Using Vitamins, Minerals, Herbs, & Food Supplements.* Garden City Park, NY: Avery Publishing Group, 1990.

Calbom, Cherie, and Maureen Keane. *Juicing for Life: A Guide to the Health Benefits for Fresh Fruit and Vegetable Juicing.* Garden City, NY: Avery Publishing Group, 1992.

Crook, William G., M.D., and Marjorie Hurt Jones, R.N. *The Yeast Connection Cookbook: A Guide to Good Nutrition, Better Health and Weight Management.* Jackson, TN: Woman's Health Connection, 2005.

Daoust, Joyce & Gene. *40-30-30 Fat Burning Nutrition: The Dietary Hormonal Connection to Permanent Weight Loss and Better Health.* Del Mar, CA: Wharton Publishing, 1996.

Hotze Health & Wellness Center. *Eating for Life: Yeast-Free Eating and Beyond.* Houston: Hotze Wellness Center, n.d.

_____. *Hotze Optimal Eating Program.* Houston: Hotze Wellness Center, 2007.

Hotze, Stephen F., M.D. *Hormones, Health, and Happiness: A Natural Medical Formula For Rediscovering Youth with Bioidentical Hormones.* Houston, TX: Forrest Publishing, 2005.

Reader's Digest Contributors, etal. *Eat Well Stay Well.* Pleasantville, NY: The Reader's Digest Association, 1998.

Robbins, Joel, D.C., M.D. *Juicing For Health: How to Restore and Maintain Optimum Health Through Juicing.* Tulsa, OK: R.W. Graybill & Company, 2001.

Rubin, Jordan S. *The Maker's Diet: The 40-Day Health Experience that Will Change Your Life Forever.* NY: Berkley Books, 2004.

Steward, H. Leighton, Morrison C. Bethea, M.D., Sam. S Andrews. M.D., and Luis A. Balart, M.D. *SUGAR BUSTERS! Cut Sugar to Trim Fat.* New York: Ballantine Books, 1995.

_____. *SUGAR BUSTERS! QUICK & EASY COOKBOOK.* New York: Ballantine Books, 1999.

Strong, James, S.T.D., LL.D. *A Concise Dictionary of the Words in the Hebrew Bible.* In Zodhiates, Spiros, ed. *The Hebrew-Greek Key Word Study Bible: Unlocking the Riches of God's Word (NASB).* Chattanooga, TN: AMG Publishers, 1993.

The Amplified Bible (AMP). Grand Rapids, MI: Zondervan, 1987.

Zodhiates, Spiros, ed. *The Hebrew-Greek Key Word Study Bible: Unlocking the Riches of God's Word (NASB).* Chattanooga, TN: AMG Publishers, 1993.

Nutrition Facts

Applesauce Muffins

Serving Size:	1 muffin
Total Servings:	12

Total Calories:	188
Fat Calories:	91
Total Fat	10.5 g
Carbohydrates	95.6 g
Dietary Fiber	5.5 g (22%)
Protein	5.5 g

Peanut Butter Balls

Serving Size:	1 ball
Total Servings:	160 (approx.)

Total Calories:	38
Fat Calories:	27
Total Fat	3 g
Carbohydrates	2 g
Dietary Fiber	0.5 g (<1%)
Protein	1.5 g

"Mom's" Squash Muffins

Serving Size:	1 muffin
Total Servings:	20

Total Calories:	150.7
Fat Calories:	93.5
Total Fat	10.2 g
Carbohydrates	17.6 g
Dietary Fiber	2.8 g (11%)
Protein	2 g

Oatmeal Bread

Serving Size:	1" slice
Total Servings:	12 (approx.)

Total Calories:	177
Fat Calories:	61
Total Fat	8.5 g
Carbohydrates	28 g
Dietary Fiber	5 g (20%)
Protein	5 g

Coconoat Flatbread

Serving Size:	2" square
Total Servings:	30 (approx.)

Total Calories:	60
Fat Calories:	19
Total Fat	3.5 g
Carbohydrates	8.5 g
Dietary Fiber	3 g (approx. 12%)
Protein	1.6 g

Nessey's Hummus

Serving Size:	2 Tbsp.
Total Servings:	96 (12 c.)

Total Calories:	32
Fat Calories:	5.4
Total Fat	<1 g
Carbohydrates	5 g
Dietary Fiber	1.3 g (5%)
Protein	2 g

Brownies

Serving Size:	2" square
Total Servings:	24

	no nuts	w/ nuts
Total Calories:	106	159
Fat Calories:	57	102
Total Fat	6.4 g	11 g
Carbohydrates	16 g	17 g
Dietary Fiber	1.5 g (6%)	2.3 g (9%)
Protein	<2 g	<3 g

Blonde Brownies

Serving Size:	2" square
Total Servings:	24

Total Calories:	203
Fat Calories:	126
Total Fat	14.6 g
Carbohydrates	20 g
Dietary Fiber	2.2 g (9%)
Protein	5.7 g

Nutrition Facts

Nessey's Nuts: Sugar 'N Spice

Serving Size:	1/4 c.
Total Servings:	5 c.
Total Calories:	227
Fat Calories:	170
Total Fat	17 g
Carbohydrates	21.3 g
Dietary Fiber	2.4 g (9%)
Protein	6.4 g

Nessey's Nuts: Texas Spice

Serving Size:	1/4 c.
Total Servings:	2 c.
Total Calories:	224
Fat Calories:	200
Total Fat	20.5 g
Carbohydrates	9 g
Dietary Fiber	2.4 g (9%)
Protein	6.1 g

"Sugar" Cookies

Serving Size:	1 cookie
Total Servings:	48
Total Calories:	64
Fat Calories:	48
Total Fat	5 g
Carbohydrates	5.6 g
Dietary Fiber	<1 g (<4%)
Protein	<1 g

Soft Peanut Butter Cookies

Serving Size:	1 cookie
Total Servings:	15
Total Calories:	147
Fat Calories:	77
Total Fat	8.8 g
Carbohydrates	20.8 g
Dietary Fiber	1.6 g (6%)
Protein	4.7 g

Nessey's Nutty Cookies

Serving Size: 1 cookie
Total Servings: 38

	no nuts	w/ nuts
Total Calories:	97	108
Fat Calories:	67	76
Total Fat	7.2 g	16.9 g
Carbohydrates	10 g	10.2 g
Dietary Fiber	1.6 g (6%)	1.7 g (7%)
Protein	3.2 g	3.7 g

Christmas Cookies

Serving Size: 1 cookie
Total Servings: 60

Total Calories:	24
Fat Calories:	10
Total Fat	<1 g
Carbohydrates	4.5 g
Dietary Fiber	0.2 g (<1%)
Protein	0.4 g

Hot Cocoa

Serving Size: 1/2 c. (4 oz.)
Total Servings: 3 (approx.)

Total Calories:	37
Fat Calories:	17
Total Fat	2 g
Carbohydrates	13.2 g
Dietary Fiber	1.2 g (5%)
Protein	1.3 g

"Tea Time" Spice Cakes

Serving Size: 2 cakes
Total Servings: 70 (approx.)

Total Calories:	92
Fat Calories:	65
Total Fat	7.5 g
Carbohydrates	7.8 g
Dietary Fiber	1.4 g (6%)
Protein	1.3 g

Nutrition Facts

Traditional Yellow Cake

Serving Size:	1 cupcake/slice
Total Servings:	12

Total Calories:	186 (w/o icing)
Fat Calories:	116
Total Fat	12 g
Carbohydrates	20 g
Dietary Fiber	3.4 g (14%)
Protein	3.4 g

Powder-Puff Frosting

Serving Size:	2 Tbsp.
Total Servings:	20

	regular	*chocolate*
Total Calories:	25	40
Fat Calories:	0	13
Total Fat	0 g	1.5 g
Carbohydrates	9.6 g	10.5 g
Dietary Fiber	0 g (0%)	0.6 g (2%)
Protein	0.3 g	0.6 g

Coco-Cupcakes

Serving Size:	1 cupcake
Total Servings:	15

Total Calories:	150 (w/o icing)
Fat Calories:	82
Total Fat	8.7 g
Carbohydrates	20 g
Dietary Fiber	3.8 g (15%)
Protein	3.6 g

5 Flavored Pound Cake

Serving Size:	1" slice
Total Servings:	9

Total Calories:	342
Fat Calories:	223
Total Fat	24 g
Carbohydrates	35 g
Dietary Fiber	4.6 g (18%)
Protein	5.2 g

Nessey's Vanilla Ice Cream

Serving Size:	1 scoop (approx. 3 Tbsp.)
Total Servings:	11
Total Calories:	178 (vanilla)
Fat Calories:	112
Total Fat	12 g
Carbohydrates	24 g
Dietary Fiber	<1 g (<1%)
Protein	1.3 g

Nessey's Heavy Cream

Serving Size:	2 Tbsp.
Total Servings:	16
Total Calories:	58 (regular)
Fat Calories:	51
Total Fat	5.6 g
Carbohydrates	2.6 g
Dietary Fiber	<1 g (0%)
Protein	<1 g

Nessey's Coco-Fudge Pie*

Serving Size:	1 slice	
Total Servings:	8	
crust:	no crust	with almond crust
Total Calories:	144	378
Fat Calories:	43	237
Total Fat	4.5 g	24.5 g
Carbohydrates	39 g	53 g
Dietary Fiber	4.4 g (18%)	7.4 g (30%)
Protein	2 g	8 g

*w/o whip cream

Almond Pastry Pie Crust

Serving Size:	1 slice
Total Servings:	8
Total Calories:	234
Fat Calories:	194
Total Fat	20 g
Carbohydrates	13.8 g
Dietary Fiber	3 g (0%)
Protein	6 g

Nutrition Facts

Nessey's Peanut Butter Pie*

Serving Size: 1 slice
Total Servings: 8

crust:	no crust	with almond crust
Total Calories:	300	533
Fat Calories:	153	347
Total Fat	17 g	37 g
Carbohydrates	45 g	59 g
Dietary Fiber	5 g (20%)	8 g (32%)
Protein	9.5 g	15.5 g

*w/o whip cream

Carrot Pie*

Serving Size: 1 slice
Total Servings: 8

crust:	no crust	with almond crust
Total Calories:	94	327
Fat Calories:	4	198
Total Fat	1.3 g	21.3 g
Carbohydrates	45 g	59 g
Dietary Fiber	1.1 g (4%)	4.1 g (16%)
Protein	2 g	8 g

*w/o whip cream

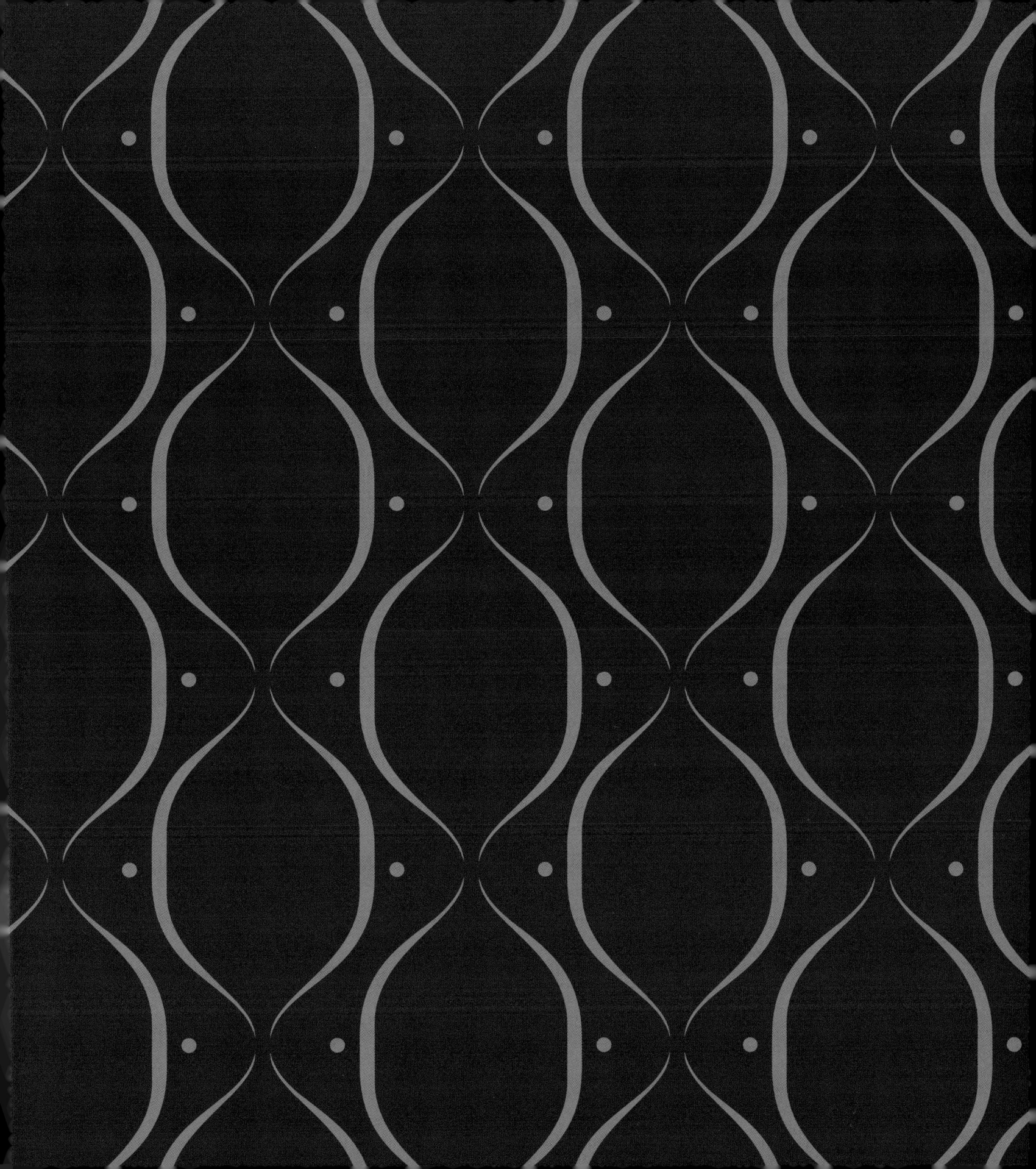

Prologue

"You have a yeast issue." It didn't surprise me, really, considering all the other health problems I had had over the last several years.

Here I was, in yet *another* doctor's office, going over some test results with my doctor, and he spoke the words with a firm compassion, leaning forward a little as he said it, his eyes locked fixedly on mine. Thus began another journey towards, hopefully, better health – perhaps another venue, through which I would finally start to "feel better."

You may be familiar with this situation, or know someone, who has been in something similar. You've seen the doctor; you've been given a load of information, medicine, etc., all "tools," which are supposed to assist you on this journey of getting your body to that lofty, "ethereal state" of "optimal health." And what's part of the package? Change your diet.

Oh, we don't like that, do we? We love eating those things like breakfast cereals, biscuits and gravy, pizza, hamburgers and French fries. But, if we are *really* serious about "getting better," something's gotta give. It ain't easy, but you know as well as I do – it's worth it.

"But do I have to sacrifice taste?! For crying out loud! Healthy food tastes so ... *healthy!*"

Well, let me put your mind at ease, my friend. Yes, sacrifice is involved when we have to change our eating habits, and it does require a great deal of determination and perseverance to stick to it; but you won't have to give up flavor, sweetness, spice, the things that make your taste buds sing and dance. I've gathered these recipes, which I have created throughout my journey toward wellness, to share

> You won't have to give up flavor, sweetness, spice — the things that make your taste buds sing and dance.

with you and assist you on your quest for better health. And, after strong encouragement from family and friends, I would like to share it all with you.

Whether you are reading this book for yourself or someone else, my hope is that you will be inspired to "run your race" with perseverance, as well as enjoy the tasty treats of *NESSIPEES*!

Introduction to Yeast-Free Eating

What is Yeast?
(in case you were wondering)

Succinctly put, yeast is a fungus that lives inside the human digestive tract, more specifically the colon, and is intended to be apart of the natural digestive system in congruence with the natural bacteria and flora also found in the colon. However, if yeast is not kept in check, it will grow rapidly, potentially causing all manner of infections and diseases. The natural digestive balance, which keeps a "rein" on the yeast, is often destroyed by the use of antibiotics, birth control pills, and many other types of medications that destroy the natural bacteria within the intestines, allowing the yeast to grow and metastasize. Unfortunately, this imbalance increases relatively quickly because yeast thrives in dark, moist environments and feeds on simple sugars, starches, alcohol, vinegar, and other fungi (such as cheese, yogurt, and mushrooms). Thus, an individual's delicate digestive balance can be drastically altered within a few days of taking any bacteria-killing medication while eating a "Normal" American diet.

This imbalance is called "Yeast Overgrowth," also known as Candida Albicans, and is typically recognized initially as primarily digestive discomforts, such as IBS, Heartburn, Gas, or Irregularity. However, if yeast continues to make its way into the digestive system unchecked, it begins to affect other factors of the body, piercing the intestinal walls, making its way into the blood stream, and resulting in issues with the immune system, blood sugar balance, and even hormone levels. Studies have shown that Candida has been linked to Chronic Fatigue Syndrome, Diabetes, Hormonal Imbalances (Hypothyroidism, PMS, etc.), Chronic Sinusitis, Allergies, and other autoimmune disorders.[1]

Well, you might think this doesn't really apply to you, and perhaps it doesn't. But if you've ever had antibiotics, have ever experienced any digestive issues, allergy problems, or other discomforts aforementioned, you might consider giving this "yeast thing" a closer look. Research has also shown that many times individuals, who started a "Yeast-Free" eating program, saw many of their health problems (such as those listed previously) resolve or greatly reduce.[2] This includes blood sugar imbalances, allergy sensitivities, digestive issues, and even Chronic Fatigue!

Now, I'm not saying Candida or Yeast is the end-all, be-all. I'm not saying all your health problems will go away just by changing to Yeast-Free eating habits. I AM saying that, it would NOT surprise me if, by eating Yeast-Free, you did experience improvements in your health in some form or capacity ... and, it would NOT surprise me if, by eating this way, you ended up feeling better, too. ☺

[1] William G. Crook, M.D., and Marjorie Hurt Jones, R.N., *The Yeast Connection Cookbook: A Guide to Good Nutrition, Better Health and Weight Management* (Jackson, TN: Woman's Health Connection, 2005), 46-54.

[2] Hotze Health & Wellness Center, *Eating for Life: Yeast-Free Eating and Beyond* (Houston: Hotze Wellness Center, n.d.), 3-5.

Introduction to Yeast-Free Eating

Yeast-Free Eating

There are many different ideas as to what a "true Yeast-Free diet" looks like. I have tried several versions of them, and have discovered that some Yeast-Free diets work better for me than others. So, I've developed a "labeling" system for my recipes that "separates" and/or "categorizes" them in accordance with their "acceptability" on what is considered "Yeast-Free."

When you begin a Yeast-Free eating program, you typically begin with what I call the "Yeast Kill" diet. This is the strictest level of a Yeast-Free program, in which you are literally "killing" the yeast overgrowth in your system by taking probiotics and antifungal medications, as well as "starving" the yeast with your eating plan.

The "YEAST KILL" Diet includes the following guidelines for what you can eat:
- LEAN Meats: Chicken, Beef, Turkey, Pork, Lamb, Venison, and Seafood
- Vegatables (except the starchy and sugary ones, like Sweet Potatoes and Carrots)
- Salads
- Dried Beans: Black, Kidney, and Red
- Eggs
- Lemons & Limes
- Avocadoes
- Cold-pressed Olive Oil
- Coconut Oil & Coconut Flour
- Black Olives
- Nuts and Nut Butters (only raw nuts and the "natural" raw butters)
- Herbal Teas
- Regular Coffees and Teas (no decaffeinated)
- Xylosweet & Sweet 'N Natural[3]

A Yeast Kill Diet excludes the following from your diet:
- Butter
- Fruit
- Oats and Oat Flour
- Milk and Milk Products (Cheese, Yogurt, Sour Cream, Ice Cream, Milk-Based dressings, etc.)
- Bread and Baked Goods (Cereals, Crackers, Biscuits, Flour Tortillas)
- Grains (Corn, Wheat, Rye, Millet, Rice, Barley)
- Pasta
- Potatoes (including Sweet Potatoes)
- Sugar (including Honey and Syrup) and Artificial sweeteners (NutraSweet, Sweet 'N Low, Equal, Splenda)
- Alcohol
- Vinegar (Pickles, Green Olives, Salad Dressings, Soy Sauce, Mustard, Mayonnaise, Ketchup, Salsas)
- Vegetable Shortening, Margarines, Partially Hydrogenated Oils

[3]Hotze Health & Wellness Center, *Hotze Optimal Eating Program* (Houston: Hotze Wellness Center, 2007), 9-13.

Sometimes Yeast Kill diets are 2 weeks long, sometimes a month. When you've completed this tough regimen, you "advance" into the "YEAST-FREE" category, in which the following can be included in the diet:
- Fruit (Except fruit juice, grapes, bananas, dried fruits of any kind)
- Butter (only real butter – NO substitutes)

Some Yeast-Free diets include Oat flour (slow-cook/steel-cut brands) but only for use in recipes. This never worked for me, so I "advanced" its inclusion into the "YEAST-FREE FRIENDLY" section, in which you have a little more liberty to add back the following:
- Oat Flour: (slow-cook/steel-cut brands only), for recipes only
- Carrots and Sweet Potatoes (in moderation)
- Grapes and Bananas (in moderation)
- Terra Chips (original ONLY)
- Rice (brown only)

I know it's hard to remember all of this, especially if you're new to the "Yeast-Free world," but hopefully with my labeling system, you will gain a better understanding of what "Yeast-Free Eating" is and, if you are actually beginning a Yeast-Free program, it will help you have a "strong start." Look for the labeling, included with each recipe:

YK: Yeast Kill
YF: Yeast-Free
Y2F: Yeast-Free "Friendly"

NESSEY TIPS:
"Nessey" appears throughout the book with different tips and ideas to aid you in your cooking process. These are my little "cooking secrets" that enhance taste, make cookies chewy, make clean-up easier, offer suggested variations for different taste sensations, etc. etc. "Nessey Tips" are not required essentials for a great recipe, only suggestions on how to improve your cooking experience.[4]

[4] The "Nessey Angel" was designed by my aunt Dianne Bianchi, who is a graphic designer. ☺

Nessey's Good Housekeeping Guide

This page is dedicated to those, who may struggle with cooking because it's a lot of work, takes a lot of time and energy, and/or it's just not your "cup of tea." I understand. I enjoy cooking, but not always, and when you don't "feel well" or are fatigued, the idea of cooking is just not very pleasant. However, I want to share some "tips" with you that have helped me to get over my happy little self, which I incorporated with my cooking experience, making it more enjoyable and "easier." I've also included a measuring guide as well, for easy reference when you're doubling a recipe, etc.

I. FIND YOUR RHYTHM
   A. When you're cooking, you need to find a rhythm that's "right for you." Not everyone has the same cooking rhythm. Some people do best if they cook first and clean up later; others clean as they go. I will give you my "cooking rhythm," just so you know how I cook and what has made cooking easier for me. Now, you can try it, but it may not "work" for you. You need to find your rhythm and stick to it.
      1) NESSEY RHYTHM: I get everything out that I'm going to use: all of my ingredients, my pots and pans, every measuring utensil, even the storage containers where the food will eventually "end up." I want everything out in front of me so I can get to it easily. Then, I "set" everything up: put out the wax paper or aluminum foil, turn on the oven, set out the paper towels, whatever. Then, I start to cook and I clean as I go (including putting everything away as I go, like the flour and/or the teaspoon). This rhythm works for me because it saves me the hassle of having to clean up later.

II. CHEW GUM or BRUSH YOUR TEETH
   A. People often complain about how they put on weight when they cook. Well, one of the reasons is we "chefs" like to "taste" our recipes as we're cooking. Bingo! Extra calories. Unless it's the first time you're making the recipe, I'd suggest chewing gum as you cook, or, if you're not a gum chewer, brush your teeth before you cook. This way, you won't "risk" eating your cookies before and after they're baked. ☺ I also drink water too, which is good for you.

III. LISTEN TO SOMETHING POSITIVE
   A. Now, not everybody can listen to something while they work. It could distract them, but there are a bunch of things you can listen to out there besides the news. I listen to Joyce Meyer's and/or T.D. Jakes's sermons, sometimes Adventures in Odyssey episodes (a radio drama series from Focus on the Family), or praise music. It keeps the atmosphere lively and joyful, and it passes the time really quickly (because you're caught up in the messages or music).

IV. WASH HANDS & WASH OFTEN
   A. Did you know that a lot of "illness" is actually the result of carelessness in personal sanitation? Yep: you forget where your hands have been, and you sure don't know what could be lurking

microscopically on the different items you touch! It's always good to wash your hands before, intermittently, and after you cook. You're handling raw eggs, organic foods, etc. You'll also be handling different seasonings, which you might inadvertently mix because your hands have remnants of another spice you used. And, should you choose not to follow "Tip #2," and you "taste" your "culinary creations" while you cook (i.e. lick your finger), just remember your mouth carries more bacteria than the mouth of a dog!

V. MEASUREMENTS:
   A. It's hard to remember all the equivalent measurements, isn't it? Here's a list for easy reference:
      1) Dash = 2 to 3 drops or less than ⅛ tsp.
      2) 1 Tbsp. = 3 tsp. (about)
      3) ¼ c. = 4 Tbsp.
      4) ⅓ c. = 5 & ⅓ Tbsp.
      5) ½ c. = 8 Tbsp.
      6) 1 c. = 16 Tbsp.
      7) 1 pint = 2 c.
      8) 1 quart = 4 c. (2 pints)
      9) 1 gallon = 4 quarts (8 pints; 16 c.)
      10) 1 lb. = 16 oz.

VI. STORING
   A. Most of my recipes use a lot of organic and "natural" ingredients. In other words: NO PRESERVATIVES. Guess what? That means the food items won't last as long. So, I ALWAYS store ALL of my food (with the exception of the nut mixes) in the fridge or freezer. Yes, even the cookies and muffins too. (I don't have to tell you what can happen if you eat "refrigerator items" that have been sitting out.) If you're using organic ingredients, you will want to properly store your completed recipe in an air tight container (like Ziploc or Glad), and in the refrigerator or freezer. (Actually, I noticed that I kinda preferred some of my treats frozen, but that's just me).
   B. Storing Time Guide:
      1) Bakery Items and Desserts
         a) 10 – 14 days in fridge; 6 – 12 months in freezer
            Exception: Peanut Butter Balls – always frozen
      2) Dips
         a) 7 days in fridge; never frozen
      3) Nuts
         a) (Raw) Always frozen – 12 months
         b) (Mixes) 2 – 3 weeks on counter; 1 – 2 months fridge; 12 months frozen

OK! There's your Nessey's Good Housekeeping Guide. HAPPY COOKING!!!

Brands®

I don't know about you, but have you ever tried a friend's or your Mom's recipe, and yours just either didn't taste quite as good, or not at all like the deliciousness you had had? Well, sometimes, this could be due to the fact that we use different brands of each ingredient. So, I decided to include a "Brands" page of the different brands I use in my recipes. Now, my tastes are going to be different than yours, so our preferences may vary. For example, you might like a certain brand of natural peanut butter over my choice, so by all means, I suggest you use THAT brand over what I've got here. This list is just another "tip" for you, if you're kinda "in the dark" on how to start, or you want to try the "original" way I made the goodies. (As a side note, some of these brands may not be available in your area anyway, so, just get what you can.)

Applesauce:
1. Organic Santa Cruz: unsweetened
2. Motts (natural: unsweetened)

Baking:
1. Baking Powder: Clabber Girl®
2. Baking Soda: Arm & Hammer
3. Cocoa: Hershey's (unsweetened)

Butters:
1. Almond Butter: Maranatha: Organic Creamy & Raw
2. Butter: Land O' Lakes Butter: Salted & Creamy
3. Cashew Butter: Arrowhead Mills Creamy or Crunchy & Roasted
4. Peanut Butter: Maranatha Organic Peanut Butter (Crunchy & Roasted)
5. Tahini Butter: Arrowhead Mills

Canned Goods:
1. Beans:
   a. Garbanzo Beans: Eden Organic (turns out fluffier in the Hummus)

Eggs:
1. Chino Valley Ranchers: Organic Omega-3 eggs
   a. Grade A – Large Brown

Flours:
1. Almond Flour: Bob's Red Mill
   a. "Finely Ground" usually

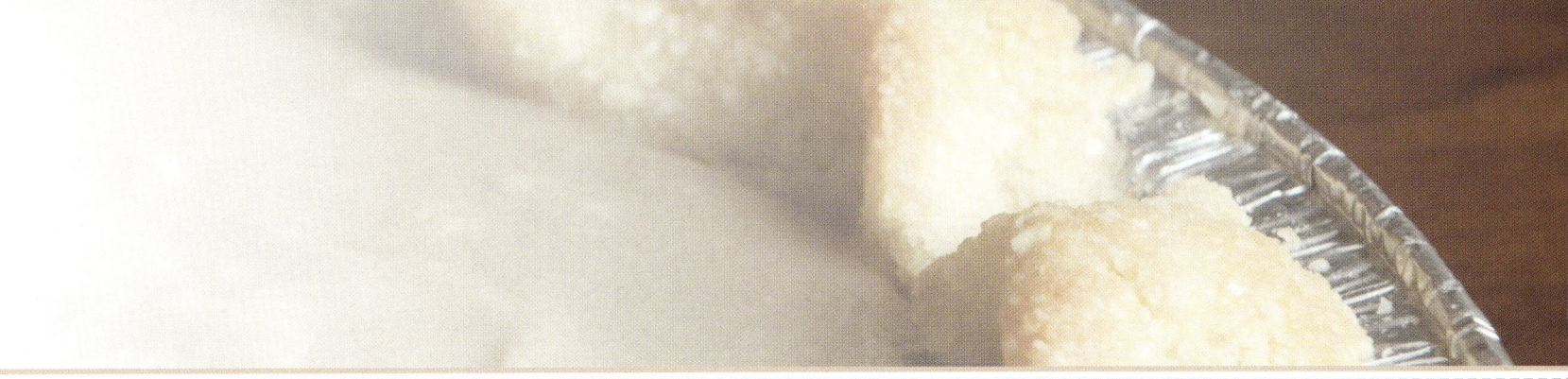

    2. Coconut Flour: Bob's Red Mill
    3. Oat Flour: Arrowhead Mills
    4. Oats: Quaker Old Fashioned
    5. Steel Ground Oats: Bob's Red Mill

Milks:
    1. Almond Milk: Blue Diamond, unsweetened
       a. Original
       b. Chocolate

Miscellaneous
    1. Lemon Juice: ReaLemon (Lemon Juice Concentrate)

Oils:
    1. Coconut Oil: Expeller Pressed Tropical Traditions
    2. Olive Oil: Hain (Extra Virgin)
    3. Safflower Oil: Lou Anna

Spices:
    1. Most every spice I use, including flavorings (vanilla extract, etc.) and salt, is either Frontier or McCormick. (I specify in the recipe, if not)
       a. Frontier is an "organic" brand found in most health food stores
    2. Salt:
       a. Sea Salt: Frontier
       b. Regular Salt: Morton Iodized

Sweeteners:
    1. Sweet 'N Natural®: found at www.physicianspreference.com
    2. Xylosweet

Water:
    1. Dasani (purified)
    2. Penta (found in health food stores)
    3. Sierra (spring water)

Acknowledgements

Wow. This is a daunting task, thanking everyone who has helped me with this book, putting it together, inspiring me to put it together, helping me with the designs, recipes, ideas, etc. etc. There are so many people, who have contributed to this project; it's hard to know where to begin, and I am certain I will leave out many. Since this is kind of a 2-in-1 book (Devotionals and Recipes) I might have to thank people separately for their help for each section.

For the Cookbook aspect of Nessipees:

First, I'd like to thank the staff at the Hotze Health and Wellness Center, who actually got me started on a Yeast-Free Eating program in October 2006, and introduced me to the new eating protocols of a Yeast-Free diet. Some of my very first recipes were inspired from some of theirs, which can be found in their book "Hotze Optimal Health Eating Program," purchased at www.physicianspreference.com,[5] and this is what got me started in creating my own.

Secondly, I'd like to thank those, who encouraged me to start this project. My parents, for actually helping me with buying the ingredients for these recipes, for eating the experiments (both successful and not), and for their love and support. My dear friends from choir, particularly Ms. Christie Kidd, Ms. LuAnn Lane, and both Mr. & Mrs. Corman, who were all recipients of some of my treats. It was Christie who actually first mentioned the idea, "You should start a cookbook," and Ms. Lane volunteered the same thought later. My "sister" Shelli, and my doctor, Dr. Tony Rector, who also mentioned the same concept, "You should make a cookbook." My grandparents, Mum & Papa Rouse and Grandma & Grandpa Harrisberger, all of whom loved my "yummies" I'd send them, and Mum (an incredible chef in her own right), truly inspired me to continue developing my "culinary" abilities. My brother and "sister-in-love," Layne and Xueling "Apple" Rouse, for also taking a plethora of recipes off of my hands (whether they wanted to or not). My Aunt Dianne, another recipient of some of my "treats," who lovingly designed a "label" for one of them, just for grins, and thus, confirmed in my mind the need to start this project (and for those of you, who don't know her, she is a graphic designer and professional artist! Her designs out of love, though not "major" to her, were tremendous pieces of artistry!) Thanks also to the WONDERFUL staff at The Life Center, for their patient and gracious acceptance of my recipes when I'd shower them with "experiments" (ranging in levels of "perfection").

In regard to the Writing/Devotional aspect:

First of all, my Dad, who has been relentless in his strong support of this pursuit, reminding me since I was in high school that I needed to keep up my writing every time I'd spout off all the things I wanted to do with my life (and forgetting to mention writing among them). Secondly, my teachers at Trinity School, particularly Mr. & Mrs. Hickman and Ms. Freeman, who also separately and repeatedly encouraged me to continue writing (while awarding me for my work). Dr. Jay Conner, one of my professors from WCC, who suggested I look into publishing some of my writings, even ones I had written for his class! My cousin, Marcus, a prolific writer (Ghostwriter) himself, who suggested I start blogging as a way to practice, an avenue I began using in 2006, and on which many of my devotionals were originally posted. To some of my fans of my blog site, particularly priests and bishops, who I don't even know, who began saying (to my parents) that I needed to write a book about my journey (right around the time others were suggesting I compile a cookbook!).

In regard to the Overall Project:

To those, who assisted me in putting this project together,

In the drafting of it: My Aunt Dianne, who designed the labels, and the "Nessey Angel," (isn't she wonderful?), Ben Blackketter, for his beautiful photography, coming over to my house to shoot these photos (and graciously accepting some of the subjects of his artistry, which I so lavishly bestowed upon him and his wife, Hilary, to consume!) Ben, my goodness! My book would have been nothing without you! For those interested in his work, you can visit his website www.benjaminblackketter.com; he is willing to travel! Matt Harnly, who worked so diligently and masterfully in designing the layout as I had envisioned it. Matt, you are a GODSEND! Working with you was a sheer delight! You are a true genius, and your level of excellence and integrity is beyond articulation! Your craftsmanship is what gave this project its character and beauty. Without you, it would have been lifeless. Bless you! My Mom, who helped me invent some of the recipes, as well as made suggestions on what to include in the book, such as my devotionals. My dear friend Leah Cavitt, who offered superb ideas, many of which I incorporated, and who nominated herself to be the "official taste-tester," though, I haven't been able to oblige her request, since she began having children!

My publishers and distributors:

Mrs. Beth O'Donnell, you were the one, who inspired me to look into the self-publishing arena! You got me started, friend! Bless you for that email! Ken Rutt, and the people of Epic Print Solutions, for helping me create Rising Monarch Press, and working with me tirelessly to ensure its beauty transferred from computer screen to reality, its excellence maintained with expert editing, and its vision realized. To Let's Face It Makeup Studio, Southlake Health and Wellness Center, Mid-Cities Community Church, Trinity School, and all the stores promoting the book (thanks to my Mom and Dad's referrals). To my Facebook friends, who have been delighted to look at my amateur photos of the recipes I've made, and pre-ordered copies of the book long before it had been drafted!

To everyone listed above, I can't thank you enough!

And now, THE Grand Finale!:

I always save the best for last. Thank You Jesus for the inspiration for this project, for the grace to complete it, for the incredible lessons of perseverance and trust that You have shown me on our road together through the valley of suffering and affliction, which preceded its existence. I dedicate this project to You, for You alone deserve all honor and glory and praise. Praise You for the joy it is to be Your servant, to love You and to serve those, whom You have placed in my path to love on Your behalf. May You be blessed by this project, which I lay at Your feet – my humble offering back to You with what You have given to me. I love You, my sweet dearest Friend. I can't wait to hug Your neck, be lost in Your arms, and feel Your tears of joy on my cheeks as we embrace for the first time on my Birthday into Your Presence. Until then, sending much love (and we'll be chatting soon).

> Thank You Jesus for the inspiration for this project, for the grace to complete it, for the incredible lessons of perseverance and trust that You have shown me.

[5]Hotze, *Hotze Program*, 9-13.

About Nessey

"Nessey," or Jenness, is an award winning author, with publications in national writing competitions, and whose devotional articles have been included in church ministerial projects.

She began experiencing severe "mysterious" health problems when she was 18, chronic debilitating issues that went undiagnosed for nearly a decade, narrowly taking her life on multiple occasions, and severely limited her ability to live independently. After 7+ years, Jenness's illness was finally diagnosed as Lyme Disease induced Adrenal Insufficiency, a rare autoimmune illness, and its effects resulted in numerous complications and additional medical conditions.

Throughout the course of her illness, however, Jenness made the most of her time and energy as best as her health would allow. She completed a B.S. in Leadership & Ministry, as well as an M.A. in Religion, with focuses in Christian Leadership and Ministry. Moreover, she participated in local and international ministry outreaches, and worked and volunteered for churches and nonprofit organizations in various ways. In addition to her ministerial pursuits, Jenness studied drama, music, and classical voice, with part of her training conducted privately in her home or via webcam when she was too ill to attend classes. In her stronger seasons, Jenness performed in local community theater shows and opera productions, even modeling and filming, all in addition to her writing and cooking.

Now, Jenness lives in New York City as she pursues her music and acting careers. To follow Jenness's progress in her professional exploits, please visit her website:

www.aboutjenness.com

OTHER TITLES BY THE AUTHOR

If you liked *Nessipees: Recipes for Life, Liberty, and the Pursuit of Wholeness*, then you will want to keep your eyes peeled for the next installment of the series:

Nessipees II: Food for Thought
(Tasting God's Sweetness from the Center of His Flame)

In *Food for Thought*, Jenness takes you on a tour of the heart as it discovers the sweetness of God's goodness from the midst of pain and frustration. Whether "spelled-out" in the honesty of prose, or gently sung in the vulnerability of her psalms, Jenness holds nothing back as she articulates what all hearts cry when their theologies and certainties fall flat and only Jesus remains. If you've ever had your doubts about a Good God in an Evil world, then this is a book for you!

But don't worry! This book's "sweetness" doesn't stop on the page! Your kitchen ovens will be blazing once again as Nessipees brings you an even LARGER variety of NEW Yeast-Free recipes, including:

- Flaky Biscuits with Strawberry Jam
- Fried Chicken and Cream Gravy
- Banana Nut Muffins
- Macadamia Nut Cookies with Icing,
- Pies, Cakes, Slushes, and much much more!

So, get your oven mitts and hearts ready!
You are in for a treat that both body AND spirit will enjoy!

Your taste buds will be dazzled, your bodies refreshed, and your spirits revived; such is the purpose and goal of the Nessipees Cookbook series.

Nessipees II: Food for Thought
(Tasting God's Sweetness from the Center of His Flame)

COMING SOON TO A STORE NEAR YOU.